SECRETS OF
ONLINE
ENTREPRENEURS

How Australia's Online Mavericks, Innovators
and Disruptors Built Their Businesses...
And How You Can Too.

BERNADETTE SCHWERDT

WILEY

First published in 2015 by John Wiley & Sons Australia, Ltd

42 McDougall St, Milton Qld 4064
Office also in Melbourne

Typeset in 11.5/14pt Rotis Serif Std by Aptara, India

© Bernadette Schwerdt 2015

The moral rights of the author have been asserted

National Library of Australia Cataloguing-in-Publication data:

Creator:	Schwerdt, Bernadette, author.
Title:	Secrets of Online Entrepreneurs: How Australia's Online Mavericks, Innovators and Disruptors Built Their Businesses... And How You Can Too.
ISBN:	9780730320340 (pbk.)
	9780730320364 (ebook)
Notes:	Includes index.
Subjects:	Successful people – Australia – Anecdotes.
	Electronic commerce – Handbooks, manuals, etc.
	Internet marketing – Handbooks, manuals, etc.
	Business enterprises – Computer network resources.
	Success in business.
Dewey Number:	658.872

Cover design by Wiley

Cover image by © retrorocket/iStockphoto.com

Printed in Singapore by C.O.S. Printers Pte Ltd

10 9 8 7 6 5 4 3 2

Disclaimer
The material in this publication is of the nature of general comment only, and does not represent professional advice. It is not intended to provide specific guidance for particular circumstances and it should not be relied on as the basis for any decision to take action or not take action on any matter which it covers. Readers should obtain professional advice where appropriate, before making any such decision. To the maximum extent permitted by law, the author and publisher disclaim all responsibility and liability to any person, arising directly or indirectly from any person taking or not taking action based on the information in this publication.

To my wonderful family
Phil, Darcy, Cameron and Maddi

And to the best parents a girl could hope for
Rosemary and David Schwerdt

CONTENTS

ACKNOWLEDGEMENTS

I would like to thank all those who made this book possible.

To the fantastic team at Wiley Publishing: Kristen Hammond, Ingrid Bond, Peter Walmsley, Clare Mackenzie, Chris Shorten and Sandra Balonyi.

To my wonderful family, friends and business colleagues: the Schwerdt Family, Heather Fraser, Judyth Wiley, Heather Albrecht, Jenny Thurlow, Karen Claren, Paul Austin, Marie Farrugia, Paula Saltalamacchia, Monique Bruggeman, Ami-Leigh O'Donnell, Georgia Power, Bridie O'Donnell, Hugh Kidman, Lynette Palmen, Meri Harli, Joanna Lawrence, Michelle West, Matt Irwin, Jan and Vic Samarias, Allan and Liz Hawkins, all the PEGS mums, Toby Tremayne, Michael Goodchild, John Skinner, Mark Farrelly, Samuel Tan, Gary Hegedus, Kelly McLaughlin, Paul McCarthy, Carson White, Harry M. Miller, Dirk van Lammeren, Marina Vaxman, Melissa Shawyer, Vuki Vujasinovic, Lynda Bredin, Belinda Tierney, Jenny Boden and David Prentice.

EXPERT ONLINE ENTREPRENEURS

- Stephanie Alexander – The Cooks Companion
- Matt Barrie – Freelancer.com
- Andre Eikmeier – Vinomofo
- Daniel Flynn – Thankyou Group
- Jodie Fox – Shoes of Prey
- Paul Greenberg – Deals Direct

- Simon Griffiths – Who Gives a Crap
- Phil Leahy – The Internet Conference
- Gabby Leibovich – Catch of the Day
- Mark Middo – The 5 Minute Business
- Kate Morris – Adore Beauty
- Tony Nash – Booktopia
- Shaun O'Brien – Selby Acoustics
- Dean Ramler – Milan Direct
- Darren Rowse – Pro Blogger and Digital Photography School
- Brian Shanahan – Temple & Webster
- Brad Smith – braaap Motorcycles
- James Tuckerman – Anthill Online
- Pete Williams – Simply Headsets, Author
- John Winning – Appliances Online

EXPERT CONTRIBUTORS:

- Kylie Bartlett – The Web Celeb
- Tim Davies – eBay
- Jordan Green – Melbourne Angels
- Jane Huxley – Pandora Radio (Australia & NZ)
- Sacha Kaluri – Australian Teenage Expo
- Sonya Karras – Australian Teenage Expo
- Valerie Khoo – Australian Writers' Centre
- Salvatore Malatesta – St. Ali and Sensory Lab
- Sandy McDonald – Get It Right Online
- Theresa Miller – Miller Ink
- Morris Miselowski – Business Futurist
- Fysh Rutherford – t20 Group
- Toby Tremayne – Magic Industries
- Belinda Weaver – Copywrite Matters
- Peter Williams – Deloitte Digital

FOREWORD

A book on entrepreneurship is exciting, but a book on entrepreneurship written by an entrepreneur, more so.

Bernadette Schwerdt is a remarkable woman. And when I heard she was writing a book, *Secrets of Online Entrepreneurs* and had asked to interview me for it, well, I jumped at the opportunity. Bernadette is a writer, yes, but she is also a formidable entrepreneur. Her copyschool business is one of Australia's most successful copywriting training companies and she has trained over five thousand people in the art of writing words that sell. Like me, and so many other entrepreneurs I have met, Bernadette has broad-view experience in the business world, including as a much in-demand public speaker, a corporate facilitator and trainer and an ad agency executive to name a few.

Bernadette has a passion for this exciting world of online entrepreneurship, one which I was fortunate to have stumbled upon in the latter part of the nineties – right place, and right time!

The entrepreneurs she has interviewed for this book reflect the broad range of people who are optimising and capitalising on the opportunities that this technology age provides. Some of the dynamic examples in this book include:

John Winning, the face of new retail in Australia, is still a young man yet runs one of Australia's most successful appliance businesses, Appliances Online, with over five hundred employees.

Tony Nash, a veteran of the internet industry was told that the online book business was doomed to failure when he launched Booktopia. And yet like the bumble bee that is technically not meant to be able to fly, Tony has built an incredible Australian book business, taking the likes of Amazon head on.

Gabby Leibovich, the founder of Catch of the Day and a disruptor to his core, has broken every rule in retail and in a few short years has built one of Australia's fastest growing retail brands.

In the Asian century, technology-led entrepreneurship is crucial to Australia's future and represents the biggest opportunity in our lifetime, but only if we take the wave. This book and the people interviewed present a candid and insightful view of what is possible for all of us. We should read this book, not only for the great stories of courage and determination and of the inevitable thrills and spills along the way, but also to rekindle our own entrepreneurial flame.

After all, it is rightly argued that in this new world we are all entrepreneurs. Whether self-employed, or in a job (entrepreneur or 'intrapreneur'), this age of disruption will challenge us all. But the good news is that disruption and opportunity always go hand in hand. The unambiguous message of this book is don't fear the wave, ride it and grab the entrepreneurial opportunities that await you with both hands and go for it! I wish you all well on your journey.

Paul Greenberg
Chairman of NORA.org.au – The Voice of New Retail in Australia
Founder of DealsDirect.com.au

THE AUTHOR'S STORY

I was born in Elizabeth, a little town about 30km north of Adelaide, South Australia. It has the dubious distinction of being regularly voted South Australia's 'most dangerous suburb'. In hindsight, this was a brilliant training ground for the argy-bargy worlds of advertising, acting and public speaking, the three pillars underpinning the mosaic of what I amusingly call 'my career'.

After watching too many episodes of the American sitcom *Bewitched*, I decided upon advertising as my career of choice, a back-up plan in case my acting career didn't work out (a wise move in retrospect).

Having completed a business degree and endured 22 years of 'Girl from Elizabeth' jokes from well-meaning friends (*What do you call a girl from Elizabeth in a white tracksuit? The bride. What's the first question to get asked at a trivia night in Elizabeth? Whaddayou lookin'at?*), I escaped...I mean...left Elizabeth for greener pastures and took up a once-in-a-lifetime opportunity to work as a marketing manager for a computer company in the United States.

Upon returning to Australia I landed the job of my dreams in shiny, happy Sydney, and became an account director and then copywriter with Wunderman Cato Johnson, the direct marketing arm of the multinational advertising agency Young & Rubicam where I worked on campaigns for Apple, American Express and Optus, to name a few.

I had a brief but formative stint as a celebrity publicist with Harry M. Miller and later achieved my gone-but-not-forgotten lifetime goal to study acting when I was accepted into the prestigious Victorian College of the Arts. Unsurprisingly, it was nothing like *Fame* and I never did get to channel my inner Irene Cara (or wear striped leg warmers and dance on car roofs), but it did lead to some fun jobs working on *Neighbours*, *Blue Heelers*, *The Games*, *Winners and Losers*, and *Jack Irish*.

I supplemented those meagre earnings with marketing consultancy, corporate training and lecturing at various tertiary institutions, including the University of Melbourne and RMIT University, and spent whatever I earned gallivanting around the world, making short films, producing and acting in plays and having a jolly good time. Just as my ovaries were reaching their 'best before' date, I stumbled upon a delightful man, who despite popular opinion, thought I'd be a good person to marry.

After having a child at the ripe old age of 40, I realised quite late in the piece that maybe a house-bound job was best for this phase of my life, so I converted my popular *Copywriting for Profit* writing training course into an online course, which kick-started a career in online entrepreneurship. As I built the business, I got to thinking: 'I wonder how all the proper business people run an online business?' so I went and interviewed them. That led to the creation of my online video series *Secrets of Aussie Online Entrepreneurs*, currently airing on *The Age* and *The Sydney Morning Herald* websites, and that show led to this book. I enjoyed writing it. I hope you enjoy reading it.

PS: I often go back to visit family in Elizabeth and to soak up the 'atmosphere'. If you're ever in the neighbourhood, stop by and say hello. Just remember to bring your flak jacket.

www.bernadetteschwerdt.com.au
www.copyschool.com

PREFACE

Being an 'online entrepreneur' means different things to different people but for me, the definition that sums it up in its purest sense is 'one who identifies a need, any need, and fills it using the internet as the main means of promotion'.

Creating an online business that sells to a global marketplace 24/7 can be intoxicating and when those first few sales arrive, it becomes quite addictive. I can still vividly recall that moment when I launched my online business. It was June 2006 and my online entrepreneurial journey had just begun.

How to make money in your pyjamas

Date: June 2006
Time: 9:17 am

The baby's napping. I'm in bed, eating Vegemite toast and drinking coffee. I fire up the laptop and check my email. My new website's been up for two days and overnight two people have bought my home-study copywriting course. One thousand, six hundred dollars went into my bank account while I slept. I forward the email receipts to my virtual assistant and she dispatches the packages to their new owners, triggering the auto-responders that will take care of all client communication for the next few months. Automation heaven! I sweep the crumbs out of the bed, put my mug aside and snuggle down to catch up on the sleep I lost tending to a newborn the night before.

I had *hoped* my new website would work, but really – *seriously* – would anyone buy my home-study course sight unseen, without even knowing me, without even so much as sending an email to check that I was real? Would they really entrust this random website with that most precious of data, their credit card?

As it turns out, yes they would and yes they did.

The thought that the average Australian would have to work a week to generate what I earned overnight was not lost on me. At that very moment, I fell in love with online business, and that thrill of seeing money go into my bank account without me having to do anything *on that day* (note the italics) still thrills me.

Online business? I was hooked.

But that was then, and this is now. Boy, how things have changed.

The allure of an online business

There was a time when online entrepreneurs were greeted with awe, curiosity and intrigue.

'Wow, someone who makes money out of thin air, without doing anything! What a talent!'

'Yes, it's a passive-income business,' we'd muse, smugly.

In the early 2000s, when the world wide web really was the wild, wild west, having an online business that delivered a passive income was not that hard to achieve. I know because I had one: a business that provided an income whether I was in bed, the Bahamas or the bath.

It seemed that if you could put a half-decent website together, devise a reasonable product and get the site on page one of Google, you really could make money out of nothing.

I recall a colleague who wrote an eBook containing original fairytale stories for children. Its point of difference was that each story ended with a simple moral that dealt with everyday childhood fears and worries. Those books are commonplace now, but back then they were the height of novelty and, even better, you could get them instantly – without going to the bookshop! Amazing. She sold more than 10 000 copies in four weeks. At $47 a pop, that's a nice little earner for a 50-page digital download.

Another colleague built a simple membership site costing $97 per month. Within a few months, he had more than 500 people in his club. That should pay his mortgage for the month.

Is passive income really passive?

Let's knock this one on the head right now.

There's no such thing as passive income. Most people I know who make money 'while they sleep' are actually really, really active in making it – they just do all the work in advance of the sale, not after it.

Passive income may look easy, and it certainly was easier to generate back then compared to now, but the reality is and always has been that you actually have to *do* something to make a passive income.

Four reasons why what worked then won't work now

The days of making easy money online are certainly not over – far from it – but you have to be a lot, lot smarter to do it. Much smarter than we were in the early days.

Why? Because in the early 2000s, four unique factors existed that enabled many novices to experience outrageous online prosperity.

- *Low competition.* If you were one of the early adopters, you could own page one of Google with no pesky competitors muddying the waters. I recall very clearly that my business had few direct competitors online when it began, and virtually none from Australia. Now, there are dozens.

- *Google was new.* Back then, search engine optimisation (SEO) was considered a dark art and if you understood even the most rudimentary SEO principles, you could get your site on page one. Now, you need to be an SEO ninja to get close, especially if your site is new.

- *People were not as savvy.* While 300-page hardcopy books struggled to sell for $30, you could sell a 60-page eBook for $60. Now, we practically pay people to download our eBooks.

- *Lower costs.* Getting a basic website up in 2006 cost well over $5000 (or whatever the web consultant figured they could get away with) so only those who were committed or had a geeky cousin in IT were prepared to invest in one. Now, basic websites are virtually free.

That's not to say you can't succeed online now because the 'conditions aren't right' – of course you can – but the point is that the conditions that existed then don't exist now. The rules have changed – dramatically – and to act as if they haven't will most certainly lead to failure.

That may sound like bad news, or like you've 'missed the boat'. But it's not and you haven't. The reality is we are living in the most transformational time in history and the potential to create a wildly successful online business has never been better. Here's why.

Why now is a great time to be an online entrepreneur

It's never been cheaper or easier to set up an online business, and the opportunities to make money from an online business have never been so plentiful.

As mentioned earlier, websites are much cheaper now; they're often even free. A personal assistant, which used to cost $4000 a month, now costs $400. A video camera, which used to cost $3000, now costs $30 per month, or it's free, depending on which phone plan you're on. A tiny newspaper advertisement that reached a sliver of the target market would cost $2000. Now it costs $200 or $20 or even $2 if you advertise on Facebook. The cost efficiencies are everywhere to be found and a cornucopia of opportunities await those who dare to dip in.

The long tail prevails

While you may not be able to sell a flimsy eBook for $100 anymore, or a piece of Jesus-shaped Nutri Grain on eBay for the price of a small Sydney unit, what you do have to sell can now be offered to a global audience. What you lose on the margin you make in the volume and it's the profitable niches within niches that are making online business very exciting.

Now more than ever your quirky little passions or hobbies can find a flourishing home online. All you have to do is create a product that helps solve a very specific problem and you've got a ready-made market that's easy to find and hungry for knowledge. For example, if you love dogs and want to create a doggy-related business, instead of focusing on dog care in general, you can drill down to create niche products like 'grooming care for labradoodles' or 'exercises for ageing labradors' or 'Halloween costumes for dogs'.

Maybe you're into naturopathy or health care for women, so instead of being all things to all women, you could focus on products and services for 'women over 40 who can't get pregnant' or 'women with alopecia' or 'gluten-intolerant women with breast cancer'.

Even if only 20 per cent, or even 2 per cent, of these markets may be interested in what you have to offer, that's still 20 per cent or 2 per cent of a global audience, and you can easily find where they reside online, which means you only pay for those you want to reach. And what's more, you know what they want so you can create a product that speaks to them directly, which means they're more likely to buy what you have.

Riches in niches

Then, of course, you've got your novelty niches like an entire cruise dedicated to vampire fanatics. Or breakable dishes specifically designed to be thrown at walls to vent your anger, miniature diapers for birds, nude wedding celebrants, and much more.

And sadly, as new lifestyle and social problems crop up, new products and services need to be created. Problem gambling has never been worse in this country, which creates the need for all sorts of products to help gamblers and their loved ones deal with the addiction and its associated problems.

Bullying, and in particular cyber bullying, has spawned an entire category of eBooks, online support groups and coaching programs for parents and teachers.

All these groups can now be found very easily online, where purchasers will eagerly devour high-quality information products and services and pay good money to get them.

It wouldn't be right to talk niches without mentioning Facebook, the preferred destination for all things weird and wonderful. Here are just a couple of bizarre Facebook groups that actually exist, which demonstrates that the 'long tail', as predicted by Chris Anderson in his book of the same name, is well and truly in force:

- *Accomplishing something before the microwave reaches :00.* Apparently, more than 1 300 000 people are obsessed about finishing some task before hearing the microwave beep. The mind boggles at the vast array of eBooks you could develop for this group, but 'get-a-life' coaching packages come to mind.

- *Dear Pringles, I cannot fit my hand inside your tube of deliciousness.* This Facebook community has more than 1 000 000 fans and is dedicated to those who can't fit their hands inside a Pringles tube. Clearly, the members of this group have oversized extremities so maybe 'big man' shoe stores or fluid-retention tablets could be the go for these poor souls. Anyway, you know what they say about people with big hands. Yeah, big gloves.

It may be harder these days to get on page one of Google. You may have to drop your prices a tad to be competitive. You will have to demonstrate some credibility to combat the onslaught of a global marketplace. You may have to work a bit harder to create quality products or services.

But when you consider the global opportunities that now exist for new, odd and eccentric business ideas, and the fact that the democratisation of information, resources and technology now enables businesses to get started within minutes, it becomes clear that the world of online entrepreneurship has truly become an Aladdin's cave of possibility. Anyone, anywhere, with even a modicum of energy and enthusiasm can become a successful online entrepreneur. Will you be one of them?

Why this, why them, why me?

When it comes to business books, I'm as inspired as everyone else about the uplifting stories told by Eric Ries (*The Lean Startup*), Ben Horowitz (*The Hard Thing About Hard Things*) and Peter Thiel (*Zero to One*).

But occasionally I've looked for books about Australian entrepreneurs and could rarely find one. Books that gave me an Australian perspective, in an Australian voice, telling me how a regular person like you or me from St Kilda or the Sunshine Coast or Toongabbie took on Harvey Norman or Coke or Elance, and won. They were the stories I wanted to read. So that, dear reader, is why I wrote this book.

Why this?

This book was written for Australian business owners, about Australian business owners, by an Australian business owner.

I chose specifically to interview Australian (and not American) online entrepreneurs for a couple of reasons. One, because we all know the back stories of those internet superstar heroes – Mark Zuckerberg (Facebook), Sergei Brin (Google), Jack Dorsey (Twitter) and Steve Jobs (Apple) – and the breathless stories of how 18-year-old Silicon Valley brainiacs barely out of high school became multimillionaires overnight by building apps that go nuts on the NASDAQ.

We know all those stories, and they're great, inspiring and uplifting, but they're *American* stories for an *American* market, a market with more than 316 million people.

We live in Australia with a tiny market of just over 23 million people, so by definition we have to do things differently. Sure, we live in a global economy and the world is theoretically 'our oyster', but for most Aussie online entrepreneurs starting out, Australia is our first port of call and, generally speaking, for all sorts of budgetary and practical reasons, the product has to work here before we start looking overseas.

> **Tip**
> We live in Australia with a tiny market of just over 23 million people, so by definition we have to do things differently.

That's why I thought it would be great to hear the stories of how some of our most famous online entrepreneurs got started: people you may not have heard of, but should hear about; people who turned an ordinary idea into an extraordinary business and made a fortune in the process, right here in little old Australia; people who started their businesses in their mum's spare bedroom, or at the kitchen table, or in the garage, and became an internet sensation. Surely they're stories worth telling, right?

Why them?

Here's just a snapshot of some of the Aussie online entrepreneur stories you'll discover within these chapters.

- Matt Barrie, co-founder of Freelancer.com, who purchased a series of websites and turned them into one of the world's most successful outsourcing marketplaces, disrupting dozens of industries in the process and facilitating global access to a host of low-cost web, IT and creative services for a fraction of their usual cost.

- Gabby Leibovich, co-founder of Catch of the Day, who started selling dresses, bags and accessories at a suburban Melbourne market, graduated to selling on eBay and is now on track to turn over $1 billion via his Deal of the Day sites.

- Jodie Fox, who combined her passion for shoes and problem feet to create one of the world's first 'design-your-shoes-online' sites (Shoes of Prey) and now has factories in China making bespoke shoes for women the world over.

- Brian Shanahan, co-founder of Temple & Webster, an online homewares shopping club, who parlayed his experience at KPMG, eBay and Gumtree to create this industry-disruptive site and now sells, among other things, more bedheads in one week than David Jones sells in one year.

- Dean Ramler, co-founder with Ruslan Kogan of online furniture store Milan Direct, who started his business with $10 000 and now has more than 300 000 customers.

- Daniel Flynn, the 26-year-old who, with his co-founders, went head-to-head with Coke to sell his bottled Thankyou Water and funnels all profits back into third-world nations, to become one of Australia's leading social entrepreneurs in the process.

- Tony Nash, co-founder of Booktopia, who transformed his internet marketing consultancy into a $40 million online bookstore success, offering a much-wanted Australian alternative to Amazon.

- Stephanie Alexander, restaurateur extraordinaire and author of Australia's favourite cookbook *The Cook's Companion*, who 'went digital' to create one of the most extensive cookbook apps possibly ever created.

- John Winning, founder of one of Australia's biggest online success stories, Appliances Online, who successfully took on the big boys of big box retailing by offering 'extreme customer service'.

- ...and many, many more.

Why me?

So why did I want to interview these people and make this information available to the wider world?

Well, the answer is simple and, quite frankly, self-serving. I wanted to find out what their success secrets were so that I could apply them to my own business, of course! And the only legitimate way to gain access to do that was to write a book. 'How devilishly devious,' I hear you say.

Sure, I could have attended a few university lectures in online entrepreneurship, or read some economic research reports, or enrolled in a masterclass with consultants (and no offence intended to university lecturers, economists or consultants — I'm two out of the three!), but when I want to know what works and what doesn't I want to get my information from those who have skin in the game.

I asked all the hard questions you would have wanted me to ask, and I followed those up with a few dozen more because I really, really wanted to know the answer to not just *why* they did it, but *how* they did it. If you don't like 'how-to' books, stop right here because this won't be for you. If you do, then read on because you'll learn how you can apply the lessons to your business too.

In addition, I've spoken at or facilitated at dozens of small-business forums, conferences and events over the past six years and I discovered that the same questions that I was asking kept coming up from the audience — questions that people simply didn't have answers to, or if they did, they didn't have the tools and techniques to implement them. Clearly, there was a massive gap between what the business books and academic theorists tell you to do, and how you actually do it!

The questions were broad in range, but they were all relevant to online business. Take a look at the few I've listed here and see if any of them resonate with you. If they do, you'll find the answer to them in this book.

Questions such as, how can I:

- build an online business?

- take my existing business online?

- turn my hobby or passion into an information product?

- turn my service into a product?

- research to find out if a topic is hot or not?

- find customers to buy my product?

- set up a website that won't cost me an arm or a leg?

- drive traffic to my site?

- source product from China?

- get an eBook made cost-effectively (and what's an eBook anyway)?

- build my database?

- get my emails read?

- source investors?

- hire a team of people to do stuff I can't do?

- know when it's time to employ staff?

- make a profit out of what I sell?

- find a point of difference that's not based on price?

- monetise my blog?

- make social media pay its way?

- compete with the cheap products from China?

...and the questions continued – these and dozens more like them.

This book also outlines in their own words how these entrepreneurs got started, why they got started, how they built their businesses, what they did right, what they did wrong, what they'd do differently and a host of other things that anyone in business would love to know about.

Like many self-made men and women, the entrepreneurs don't look back to kick over the traces of how they've done it — they're too busy getting on with it — so I did the kicking over instead.

I interviewed the entrepreneurs at length, many of them more than once. I visited some of them at their offices, their factories and their warehouses and saw their businesses in action and their people at work. I looked at what they did, how they did it and how they interacted with their staff. I compared what they did with the way other entrepreneurs do things. I looked for the patterns of behaviour, the questions they asked of themselves, their staff and the business, the assumptions they made and the risks they took. I looked at what they did that others don't do. I found out what they valued and what they didn't; what they measured and how they managed it.

What I received was a fascinating, privileged insight into the worlds of some of Australia's most successful and innovative businesses — and the reasons why they are successful. Those reasons are to be found in this book.

When I asked Darren Rowse, one of my interviewees and founder of ProBlogger (www.problogger.net), why he started his blog (a blog that has gone on to attract more than five million readers per week), he said he 'wrote the blog he wanted to read'.

Well, I wrote the book I wanted to read.

I hope it's a book you want to read too.

INTRODUCTION

> Hell, there are no rules here – we're trying to
> accomplish something.
>
> *Thomas A. Edison*

The state of play

It's Friday night. It's hot. The kids are swimming in the pool.

The mums, sipping wine, are gathered around the white stone-top bench, a feature in almost every middle-class, suburban Australian household. They're nibbling on crackers, dip and cheese, musing over the week that was.

Michelle, the owner of the house, is scrolling on her iPad, distracted.

'What are you looking for?' I ask.

'A dress. I've just been invited to the races tomorrow and I want something new to wear.'

'The shops will be shut in one hour's time,' I say helpfully.

'I know. I'll buy it from this online store in South Melbourne,' she responds, sliding the iPad over to me.

'They deliver within the hour and I can return it if it doesn't fit and get another one sent over, free of charge. Not bad, huh?'

'Really?' I murmur.

'Yeah, I use them all the time. You should check them out. I'll email you the link.'

That conversation, and millions like it, is being held all over the world in kitchens, coffee shops, bars, pools and pubs, and they're not just talking about a dress, but everything that we use and consume in our daily lives.

And it's conversations like this that make traditional retailers nervous. Very nervous.

Who's *not* shopping online?

When people like Michelle—a conservative, middle-aged woman with a passing familiarity with computers—migrates to shopping online, bypassing the traditional high-street traders that have been the go-to fashion portal of choice for women like her for decades, what does it mean for those who've invested their life's work and staked their retirement on building up and then selling their one- or two-store retail empire? How can they compete in a global market without killing themselves (figuratively speaking, of course) in the process?

The digital natives—the kids in the pool—have already migrated. No hope there.

So who's left to prop up the high-street traders and the hard-top shopping malls? Is it the people like my mother—the 'grey nomads'—those from the frugal generation who've resisted online shopping but who now just happen to be the fastest growing users of Facebook? What happens when people like my mother abandon the high-street mall due to old age, overpriced lattes, tricky knees and taxis that don't turn up, and seize upon the convenience that online shopping provides? What then?

Will that be the proverbial 'nail in the coffin' that condemns these long-suffering high-street traders to oblivion?

No industry is immune

Of course, it's not just the retailers who are suffering. Services are suffering too.

Creative providers such as web designers, app developers, copywriters, graphic designers, coders, animators and editors are all feeling the pinch as educated consumers turn to outsourcing sites that provide the same, if not better, service at a fraction of the cost.

Bookkeepers, lawyers, accountants, admin assistants...they too are feeling the crunch from the online providers popping up to offer services that cut deep into the ever-diminishing margins of these 'professional service providers'.

Ethics aside as to whether we should engage with poorly-paid (by Western standards) outsourcing providers based in the developing world, the reality is people *are*. And there is no doubt the demand for these services is growing.

The kids will be all right. Or will they?

Once online shopping really hits critical mass (it hasn't even touched the sides yet in Australia), how will it change the way we and, perhaps more importantly, our children live?

Where will our children get that all-important work experience that we got at Big W, Dad's office or Uncle John's car yard?

Where will they learn those tough but necessary lessons we've all had to learn about how to deal with the bad bosses, broken promises and borderline sociopaths who populate most companies (and who seem to pop up with surprising regularity in Finance and HR...or is that just me?).

What will become of our local street culture when every third shop in the main streets of every suburb displays that harbinger of doom: the 'for lease' sign? What will replace the video shop, the toy store, the book shop, the dress shop, the shoe shop? Another coffee shop? A tanning salon? A dog wash? What careers can our children look forward to? Baristas for life? Nail-bar veterans? Pick-and-packers at a drop-ship warehouse?

If we're not part of the solution, are we part of the problem?

But before we go too much further, and before you judge me to be an armchair critic of online consumerism, I must declare that I am, without question, part of the problem.

I too like to snag a cheaper product if I can.

I too like the convenience of paying a bill online.

I too like to avoid the rush-hour commute to pick up a birthday present.

A local Melbourne council asked me to write and produce a 'vox pop'-style video for their website to encourage local business owners to buy local rather than shop online. That very same evening, I conducted a small-business forum for hundreds of the *same* business owners exhorting them to embrace the digital era and start thinking globally. The irony was not lost on me.

But aren't we all facing the same conundrum?

We want to support our local toy shop, but when the same toy costs 20 per cent more from them than it does online, well, what are we to do? Take a bullet for the entire Australian economy in the hope that everyone else will too? Fat chance. In today's tight economy, a 20 per cent premium is too much to pay for supporting a local store, even if the toy does come gift-wrapped.

We all want our children to have satisfying jobs, full-time employment and the benefits of a flourishing economy.

But does it mean they have to study the STEM subjects (science, technology, engineering and maths), in which they have no interest, in order to stay relevant in a borderless marketplace that cares nought for race, creed or colour?

Why can't things be the way they were?

I've met thousands of business owners at my small-business marketing workshops and forums, and for a small but significant cross-section, they all have one thing in common: the hope that things will just 'return to normal', the way they used to be, whatever that was. But there *is* no normal anymore, and it's become quite clear that to keep a business afloat in the global marketplace today, and with the 'internet of things' upon us, the pace of life for them is about to pick up, not slow down.

> **Tip**
> Don't force your kids to do school subjects they don't love just so they get a job in the future. Just make sure they do either science, technology, engineering or mathematics (STEM).

This resistance to embracing the digital age is embedded in the faint hope that we can hold onto the control we used to have. Control over the customer. Control over the conversation. Control over our destiny. But we can't. Control is gone, forever…if we ever had it at all.

What's the future of business, any business?

There is hope. And it comes from someone who knows: Paul Greenberg, executive director of NORA (National Online Retailers' Association) and co-founder of Deals Direct (www.dealsdirect.com .au), Australia's first online department store and one of Australia's first big online success stories. His expertise lies in the area of retail, and whether we like it or not, we are all retailers no matter what we sell, so his advice is pertinent for all businesses. He firmly believes that the days of the pure-play retailers—those with no physical presence—are coming to an end, and that signals good news for everyone, especially the retailers at the coal face. Paul says:

> Customers are rewarding multiple touch points so I'm afraid even the pure player online needs to start looking at some physical

presence. Arguably the sweet spot for the new retailer is the intersection between the physical and the digital world. This will be the Holy Grail for the next few years in my view.

Sometimes we want to shop online, sometimes we want to shop on our mobile device, and it's this increased mobility that's changing the rhythm of retail. Sometimes we want to come into a store and commune, to have a look, have a bit of a touch and feel. Sometimes I want to come to a warehouse and pick up my stuff if I make a big order.

As a retailer you need to ask, 'How can I reasonably, efficiently and profitably provide multiple touch points to the customers?' I think those retailers that are engaged in the journey will continue to thrive.

What's Gucci doing?

It's instructive to notice what early adopters and trendsetters like the European fashion houses do when it comes to combating the threat of online retail. Luxury brands such as Balenciaga, Louis Vuitton, Gucci and Prada – and closer to home, Sass & Bide, Bassike and Dion Lee – are clearly leading the charge here in creating not just multiple touch points but in-store multisensory experiences. We can clearly learn from what they're doing, and either adopt their strategies or at least modify them for our budgets and keep the essence of the lesson.

> As a retailer you need to ask, 'How can I reasonably, efficiently and profitably provide multiple touch points to the customers?'
>
> Paul Greenberg

These temples of luxury are no longer just backdrops to the clothes or places for dresses to hang, but immersive branding experiences designed to offer customers a money-can't-buy event that online shopping can never provide.

Paul Greenberg of Deals Direct says:

> The architecture, lighting, fit-out and layout of the luxury boutique is now a star in its own right, and plays an integral role in the storytelling behind the brand's artistic integrity and, importantly, delivers a 'sensory experience' that cannot be delivered online.

This experience of touching, trying and smelling an object can never be replaced and while many of the larger chains are struggling to implement change, these high-end brands are taking it to another level.

Whereas shopping used to be considered something you *had* to do, now it's a form of entertainment for the whole family, almost replacing the role that Sunday church once played. Paul says:

The mall has morphed into a destination rather than a stop-along-the-way: the public face of the brand and a place where art installations, curated exhibitions and windows featuring live action are commonplace.

Andy Warhol was right

In the 1960s, artist Andy Warhol famously predicted that all department stores would become museums and all museums would become department stores, so it's interesting to witness the National Gallery of Victoria and how its museum shop now collaborates heavily with leading local and international artists, designers and makers to offer unique contemporary products.

And in a sublime counterpoint, many of Sydney's arty set will recall French luxury brand Hermès bringing its travelling exhibition 'Festival des Metiers' to the Museum of Contemporary Art, giving visitors the opportunity to watch eight Hermès craftsmen execute their work firsthand for free. These included an up-close demonstration of the famous Hermès silk scarf printed right before their eyes, and the chance to meet the leather craftsmen who make the brand's renowned Birkin bags.

An online walk-in store

Consider Sneakerboy, a walk-in online store based in Melbourne that displays a large range of sneakers from high-fashion labels such as Balenciaga and Givenchy, to special limited editions by Adidas and Nike. Yes, you read correctly. An online store you can walk into. There's no stock, no cash, no till and no product to take home. All that's needed to make a purchase in the store is a smartphone (or one of the in-store iPads) and a Sneakerboy ID. The rest of the available space is dedicated to the range of shoes, which means Sneakerboy can boast a larger range of stock on a much smaller footprint.

Sneakerboy Melbourne is at the cusp of this retail revolution and even pure-play retailers such as eBay are getting in on the experiential act. Not too long ago, I was in Sydney at Circular Quay when eBay had a pop-up store on the foreshore, with fully decked-out kitchens, bedrooms and lounge rooms stocked with eBay items for sale. Each room contained actors – a teenager in his bedroom playing guitar, a middle-aged couple in the kitchen cooking a cake, two young girls playing with a dollhouse – while staff in eBay shirts strolled around, iPad in hand, to help out those who saw something they liked so they could buy it then and there.

While not everybody will like where retailing is headed, the fact remains that existing bricks and mortar have to accept that change is inevitable.

Paul Greenberg says:

> The pure-play days are over. Multichannel is the way to go. In fact, we shouldn't even refer to them as 'channels' any more. It's a multiple touch-point model. It's the 'new retail'.

This is good news for everyone, especially the retailers on the high street. They may not like where retail is headed but they can at least take comfort from the fact that the rumours of the death of retail are exaggerated.

Paul adds:

> The future can be bright for retailers, but they have to start changing their ways, their thinking and outlook. They have to think local but act global, and they have to embrace the digital age with gusto.

Today, the future of business is online business. And, just quietly, the title of this book is out of date already. It was before I even started writing it. You see, there is no online business. There's just business. We're all online, but as in *Animal Farm*, some of us are just more online than others.

The 7 steps to creating a wildly successful online business

You can't conduct in-depth, probing interviews with dozens of online entrepreneurs without learning something; without seeing some patterns at work and similarities in the way they operate. In fact, what I discovered is that there are seven basic steps involved in the creation of an online business. Yes, this is a complete oversimplification and the claim does not do justice to the immense skill it takes to operate a business. But, on a very simplistic level—and I use my own online business as the template—you can see that when you overlay these seven steps onto any online business, the model stacks up. Let me demonstrate them using my own online business as a model.

As you will see, when I built my online business, it was as a result of a random series of steps that were in no way, shape or form planned, ordered or considered. The business succeeded more due to good luck than good design. However, in retrospect I can see that I was in fact doing 'all the right things', even if I didn't know it.

In my example of the seven steps I'll outline the principle and give a brief overview of what the principle means. Then I'll describe how I inadvertently followed that principle when I built my business.

I believe this 'overlaying' approach will assist you in your business because it's easier to see how this model works for a simple business than a complex business, but the principles remain accurate and relevant no matter what size or type of online business you run. You'll also see how the entrepreneurs used this same seven-step pattern to build their businesses, which is why the book is presented in seven chapters. Each chapter represents a separate step.

7 steps to creating a wildly successful online business

Here's a seven-step process for creating, building and operating a successful online business.

Step 1: Purpose

You need to get clear on the 'why'. What is your reason for wanting an online business? When you've got your first answer, ask 'why' again, and then ask it again. Asking the '3 whys' really gets you to the nub of why you want or need something.

My 'why' was very clear. I wanted a lifestyle business to replace the income I had foregone as a result of choosing to be a stay-at-home mum, and to have a portable business that could be accessed from wherever I was. My 'why' was also deeply important on a personal level. If my online endeavour didn't work, I would have had to travel extensively in order to run my consulting and training business—something I didn't want to do.

Tip: It really helps to have a burning 'passion' behind wanting an online business. Without it, the inevitable headaches, hassles and heartache could lead you to give up, accept defeat and say, 'It's just not worth it'. Find a reason that matters deeply to you.

Step 2: People

You need to build a team around you that will support your vision, provide expertise you don't have and hold you accountable.

I had my small but trusty team of contractors who helped me build the business: a virtual assistant (VA), a graphic designer, a web developer, a printer, a videographer, a video editor, a photographer and the obvious support staff such as accountants. In addition, I had my clients, who had already bought the product before it was finished (more about this in chapter 3). What they did was hold me accountable. Without that pressure to finish the product (from people who had already bought it but had not been given the full product) it's quite possible I would have given up on the project entirely. Either commit yourself financially to the project so that there's no backing out, or commit yourself emotionally (to your clients, or in a public statement) to ensure that you step up and make it happen.

Step 3: Planning

You need to be confident in what you're selling: that it has a market, that the prototypes work and that testing has been conducted using a Minimal Viable Product (MVP) that real people have paid real money for.

Little did I realise, but I had been testing my online offering via the face-to-face courses I had been running for years. I had built a substantial database. I had run the short courses so I knew who was in my target market. I had tested the content, and I knew what worked and what didn't. I had bootstrapped the business and knew that investing further in creating an online version of it was a gamble that was likely to pay off.

Step 4: Profit

You need to know that what you're offering has a target market that's able and willing to pay your price, that the demand for what you offer is in a growth phase, that you're not differentiated by being the lowest priced, and that it is difficult for others to easily replicate what you do.

Unbeknown to me, copywriting was about to become a boom business due to an explosion in the need for websites, blogs and online content. Equally unknown to me was the fact that it was very difficult to access copywriting training unless you worked in the advertising industry. As a result, demand for my product was high and competition was minimal. Also working in my favour was that the product was not easily compared with others vis-a-vis its price or its content, so my success was based on how well I could write the copy and position the concept of becoming a freelance copywriter. Equally important was the fact that my expenses were low (just printing, some

(continued)

7 steps to creating a wildly successful online business (cont'd)

contractor work, web hosting and my time delivering the coaching calls to my students), enabling me to maximise my profit.

Step 5: Positioning

You need to demonstrate credibility, provide third-party proof that you are as good as you say, answer every question the customer has about the product (before they buy it), make it easy for them to buy, offer an iron-clad money-back guarantee and prove that you are a real business with real premises.

This was my strong suit. I had a library of video testimonials from happy clients I had filmed at my face-to-face courses. I was endorsed by industry associations. I had a 100-per-cent money-back guarantee. I had an extensive FAQ on my website, loads of resources and blogs that I had written to demonstrate my expertise and the physical evidence that I was a going concern: a landline phone number, a street address, an email address and photos of me, my events, my students, and more.

Step 6: Profile

You need to have an online identity that reflects who you want to be and how you want to be seen, great content that operates 24/7 selling your business while you can't, and a website that ranks well on Google.

I was on page one of Google for my preferred search terms, the absolute jewel in the crown that made my business so successful early on. I had loads of speaking engagements, which helped increase my profile while I was building my database. I had videos of myself on YouTube. I was blogging for others and had marketing columns in industry magazines and online journals.

Step 7: Promotion

You need to be able to market your business using PR, print, social media, events, email and content marketing and a

> *raft of free resources to offer in exchange for the prospects' contact details.*
>
> I had a good, strong website with lots of content and strong backlinks to reputable organisations. I got extensive PR through sheer luck and timing and received highly positive news stories. I wrote persuasively, and I wrote often: emails, blogs, stories, video scripts, slide decks. I had a big database with a robust CRM system and wrote segmented emails to different audiences to match their needs. I was creating content before the word 'content' even existed as a marketing term. Salesmanship in print.
>
> Imagine what I could have done if I had known what I was doing!

So there you have it. My self-styled seven-step process, which I found, retrospectively, worked very well for me. When I overlay those seven steps on the businesses of the entrepreneurs I've interviewed, the model stands up well.

The purpose of this outline is to 'shine the light' on the steps I and others have taken to bring an online business into reality. You may have already started your business, but you might see that you're missing one or two steps. Maybe you've already got a successful offline business and you want to retrofit the steps to fit where you're at.

Or maybe you're just starting out and you have a clean slate to start with. You can attack it in any order that makes sense to you. There is no right way to do it, but here's a small tip: you'll get better results if you follow all the steps in the prescribed order.

So here's your chance to get started. Your first step awaits you: finding your purpose. Why do you really want an online business? Take a look at how some of Australia's most successful online entrepreneurs found their vision and purpose and how they translated that into actionable steps to get their business off the ground.

Tip

There is no right way to do it, but you'll get better results if you follow all the steps in the prescribed order.

CHAPTER ONE
PURPOSE

> One half of knowing what you want is knowing
> what you must give up before you get it.
>
> *Sidney Howard*

What's your vision?

There was a boat docked in a tiny Greek village. A man in a business suit complimented the Greek fisherman on the quality of his fish and asked how long it took him to catch them.

'Not very long,' answered the fisherman.

'But then, why didn't you stay out longer and catch more?' asked the businessman.

The fisherman explained that his small catch was sufficient to meet his needs and those of his family.

The businessman asked, 'But what do you do with the rest of your time?'

'I sleep late, fish a little, play with my children and take a nap with my wife. In the evenings, I go into the village to see my friends, have a few glasses of ouzo, sing a few songs and dance all night...I have a full life.'

The man interrupted, 'Sir, I have an MBA and can help you. You should fish more, and with the proceeds buy a bigger boat. In no time you could have several boats and eventually you would have a fleet. Then, instead of selling your catch to the middleman, you could sell directly to the consumers. You can then leave this little village and move to Athens, London or even New York City! From there you can direct your huge enterprise'.

'How long would that take?' asked the fisherman.

'Twenty, perhaps 25 years,' replied the man.

'And after that?'

'Afterwards? That's when it gets really interesting,' answered the businessman, laughing. 'When your business gets really big, you can start selling online to an international audience, launch an IPO and make millions!'

'Millions? Really? And after that?'

'After that you'll be able to retire, live in a tiny village near the coast, sleep late, fish a little, play with your children and take a nap with your wife. In the evenings, you can go into the village to see your friends, have a few glasses of ouzo, sing a few songs and dance all night...you can have a full life.'

What do you want? Easy to ask. Hard to answer.

Do you want a home-based business that fits in around the school pick-up hours, that delivers the income level you need and that gives you the freedom to do as you please, when you please, with whom you please?

Do you want a multimillion-dollar, publicly listed start-up that gets you on the cover of the *BRW* magazine Rich List edition, sees you jetsetting around the world and provides a glittering lifestyle to match?

Maybe you've already got a successful business and you just want to incorporate some smart online strategies that will increase your revenue without increasing your costs.

Whatever your vision for creating an online business, what's important is that you understand *why* you're doing it and *what* you want from it.

Make a decision: lifestyle vs equity

> Many men go fishing all of their lives without
> knowing that it is not fish they are after.
>
> *Henry David Thoreau*

The Greek fisherman referenced in the opening story certainly knew what he wanted.

In online terms, he had what's known as a 'lifestyle business'.

Conventionally speaking, lifestyle businesses typically have limited scalability and potential for growth because such growth would destroy the lifestyle for which their owner-managers set them up. But for those who want to live a certain lifestyle – one that fits in with their family, that enables them to live near the beach (and drink ouzo for lunch and have a siesta with their wives) – or who just want to create a part-time income while they work full time elsewhere, then a lifestyle business is a fantastic and not-to-be-scoffed-at objective.

This of course is in contrast to an equity or growth business, where the owner intends to build real assets with a tangible value that can be bought and sold either as shares or as the entire business. Success to a business owner of this nature would be defined as the increase in value of the business over time.

These are very different scenarios. 'Equity' or 'lifestyle' is a fundamental decision you need to make when you're starting out.

What's important is that you do it consciously. I built my online business unconsciously. I didn't have a plan and I wasn't working to a system that would guarantee an outcome. Reflecting on the interviews I conducted with the entrepreneurs for this book, I can see that some of them (but certainly not all) did not have a vision for their business at the outset either.

At some point, however, each entrepreneur had to make a decision: to invest in the business and grow – hire staff, seek investors, rent premises and dig in for the long haul – or to acknowledge it's a lifestyle business and be happy with the level of income that generates.

If you're contemplating going into business with a partner, determine whether you would both answer the same way. Neither is good or bad. It's just, which one is for you?

Like the Greek fisherman, know your outcome before you begin.

Key questions to consider before setting up your online business

Before you launch into creating an online business, or even amending an existing business to make it more online savvy, there are a number of questions you need to consider. By answering these in advance, you will save yourself a lot of time and effort.

- What's the best business model for you?

- Should you follow the passion or the profit?

- What will you sell?

- What problem are you solving?

- Should you start with the end in mind?

- What business are you in?

- What challenges should you expect?

- Should you give up your day job to get it started?

What's the best business model for you?

Do you want a lifestyle business or a growth business?

Paul Greenberg, co-founder of Deals Direct, Australia's first online department store, has this to say:

> You must be very clear about what you are looking for from the business. Is it a lifestyle business, or do you want to develop world domination and take on Amazon? There is a view in this new economy that you need to get big or you need to get out. That you have two choices: go for growth or find a niche that's underserviced. What's most important, however, in my opinion, is 'to thine own self be true'.

Kylie Bartlett, author of the best-selling book *Friends with Benefits*, has a very clear vision for her business.

> I built a very successful corporate training business that had 25 staff and turned over millions, but now I know one thing: I don't want staff! I'm a gypsy. I want a lifestyle business that enables me to travel when and where I want, and work from a beach, a café or a car. I don't want the hassles of turning up to an office every day and managing people. My online business supports my lifestyle, not the other way around.

Matt Barrie, co-founder of the world's biggest outsourcing marketplace, Freelancer (www.freelancer.com), has a very different viewpoint.

> Don't think about building a business that's going to be a lifestyle business. Think about a business that's going to be in a billion-dollar-plus market because if you miss then you've still got a good opportunity to do well. But if you aim for a niche market it's sometimes a struggle. And the internet is so scalable. There's two billion people on the internet so if you get some success, it can take off quite quickly. Like Pinterest,

Tip

Think big. If you fail, you've still got a chance of succeeding.

which is really just scrapbooking online and a pretty simple concept, which came out of nowhere to be the sixteenth biggest website on the internet in one year. So there is opportunity out there.

Getting clear about the sort of business you want to run is one of the first steps towards creating a successful online business.

Passion or profit: what should you follow?

Now that you've thought about the scale of the business you want to build, it's time to consider what you'll sell.

Sell what people want: 'go for the cash'

Booktopia (www.booktopia.com.au) co-founder Tony Nash recalls a formative experience at a business conference held by business motivator and author of *Rich Dad Poor Dad*, Robert Kiyosaki:

> Robert instructed us to try and sell our service to anyone and everyone at the conference. If someone bought our service, we got $1. That was a big win. I was selling recruitment services at the time. I put my best suit on, went out and pitched like a pro. Not one sale. I went out the next day, but I changed my strategy. I became 'smooth Tony'. I listened, I reflected back, I built rapport. No luck. 'Tony,' they said. 'We'd love to give you $1, but there's only one problem: we don't need what you're offering.'

Annoyed at his lack of success, Tony changed his tack and offered 3-minute massages for $1, having trained as a masseur in an earlier life.

Tony exclaimed:

> I was inundated! I made $14 in the 45 minute session! I was rich! But I had also learned a valuable lesson: sell what people want. You've got to go for the cash! You've got to work out, what am I selling? What will people give me money for? What have I got that people will want in exchange for their cash? If they're not giving you money for your product, you need to change it. Do something. Offer something else.

It often comes down to this very simple question: Should I follow my passion or should I follow the profit? This is important because it fundamentally determines what you'll sell and how you'll sell it. It dictates the foundation upon which the entire business is built.

That's not to say that passion and profit are mutually exclusive. Far from it. But it's a very important decision because people with an evangelical passion for their product or service often blindly enter into a market thinking their burning

> If they're not giving you money for your product, you need to change it. Do something. Offer something else.
>
> Tony Nash

fervour will eclipse all the commercial concerns that go along with creating a new endeavour. And they fail to ask the most basic questions:

- Is the market already crammed with competitors?

- Why will they choose me?

- What have I got to offer that's better, cheaper or different?

- What happens if a competitor opens up next door or online?

- What can I offer that is unique?

- Have I got the marketing ability to sell whatever it is I'm making?

- Is there an audience willing to pay me money for what I've got to offer?

In my experience, confusion and indecision surrounding the right or best business idea to pursue is the number-one reason why people fail to get started; they simply can't

Tip
Sell what people want, not what you want to sell.

make up their minds about what they want to sell and if they do, they don't have the tools or know-how to validate it to give themselves the confidence they need to press on.

Which path should you take?

Paul Greenberg believes that building a business around a passion can be instructive.

> If you create your online business around a hobby, a pastime or a sport, it will help make the inevitable failures easier to deal with. If you're not super passionate and enthused about your product, service, industry or category, then when the waves crash and you're thrown for a six, it's going to be harder to get back up.

Passion pursuers

Kate Morris from Adore Beauty (www.adorebeauty.com.au) knows about building a business on passion. As a young woman living in Tasmania, she loved makeup but couldn't get the brands she wanted, so she set about building an online store to stock makeup so that anyone, anywhere, could buy the brands they knew and loved. She was driven by a youthful passion to build her business, which was just as well, because few brands would come on board at the outset and it took her many years to get it to a point where it would become a formidable competitor to other beauty outlets. But her persistence and naïvety paid off. She tells of her first appointment with Natalie Bloom, founder of Bloom Cosmetics, to get her on board as a supplier.

> I came into the meeting to convince a major brand to come on board with us and I had nothing to show her. I didn't know that I should have had a proposal and spreadsheets and projections! I look back now and laugh, but at the time I was mortified at how naïve I must have seemed. She was very gracious about it and gave me some advice which I've never forgotten—bring a proposal! I was very unprepared to set up an online business. I didn't have any money in the bank, I had no experience in online marketing, I knew very little about business yet I know it was my passion for the product that got me over those early hurdles.

Daniel Flynn, co-founder of Thankyou Water (www.thankyou.co/water), was driven by a burning passion: to help others live a longer life.

> I recall seeing a documentary where a young boy in a developing country brought back water from the village well that was poisoned. He gave his little brother the water to drink and the boy subsequently

died from drinking the water. I wondered how that brother felt being the one to give his little brother the water that killed him. I was so upset at that story, and I imagined how I would feel if I did that to my brother and how terrible that would feel, and I just knew I had to do something that would help. That's when I came up with the idea of selling something that we all use, but giving people the knowledge that if they bought *our* water the proceeds would go towards helping others. Even when things get tough with the business, all I have to do is remember that story and it puts everything in perspective.

> **Tip**
>
> A word of warning: You sometimes lose a good hobby when you turn it into a business.

For social entrepreneur Simon Griffiths, a deep-seated desire to also help others less fortunate saw him start his business Who Gives a Crap (www.whogivesacrap.org), a toilet paper manufacturer that uses 50 per cent of its profits to build toilets in the developing world.

The business got started because we saw there was a huge sanitation problem globally. About two-and-a-half billion people are without access to toilets, which results in diarrhoea-related diseases that fill half of the hospital beds in sub-Saharan Africa and kill about two thousand children every single day.

I trained as an engineer and an economist and realised pretty quickly that I could do the corporate work and do it really well, but I just didn't really feel that passionate about it, and as a result I wasn't ever taking work home with me, which for me didn't feel right.

What I realised is that I was incredibly passionate about problem solving and working with innovation, but I still had this very strong pull to the developing world and I wanted to work on social problems.

So I realised that I had to do something that had the outcomes that I cared about but included the process of problem solving and the innovation that I loved. That's how I got started.

Darren Rowse, founder of ProBlogger (www.problogger.net) and Digital Photography School (www.digital-photography-school.com), was simply following his passion for writing and photography and had no idea at the time that this combination of talents would one day generate a worldwide audience of five million readers.

> I think I was lucky, or smart, depending on how you look at it, in terms of the topics that we've done. We started writing about photography just before it began to boom as an industry. It was when everyone was getting cameras on their phones and digital photography was taking over from film, so it was a good time to be writing on that topic.
>
> The same with blogging. When I started ProBlogger it was just when people started to think about blogging commercially. So partly it was timing and it's something that I've stuck with as well. I love writing and it's not a chore. I have been blogging for 12 years and I can't think of too many days where I wouldn't have published something in that time.

Kate Morris from Adore Beauty has seen a lot of businesses come and go over the years.

> I see people start businesses for all kinds of wrong reasons. Yes, you should obviously start a business to make money but really you should start a business because of something you feel really passionate about. There are going to be really hard times and if you're not passionate about your product and care for it deeply, then you won't really know how to communicate with your customers. How will you keep going if it's not something that excites you?

Profit players

Pete Williams, master online strategist and co-founder of the online retailer Simply Headsets (www.simplyheadsets .com.au), online telecommunications company Infiniti (www .infinititelecommunications.com.au) and many other businesses, doesn't really mind what he sells. It's not that he doesn't care; it's just that he knows that his finely tuned sales and marketing system can sell anything.

> It's okay to pursue your passion, but you've got to have a system to market it. Irrespective of what you sell, if you can't sustain it with passion, you'll need to sustain it with results.

For Brian Shanahan, co-founder at Temple & Webster (www. templeandwebster.com.au), deciding to enter the online homewares market was strictly a numbers game.

Brian: When I was CFO at eBay Australia and then later as MD of Gumtree International, I saw that there was significant demand for product in the homewares and furniture category but there were very few online retailers meeting this demand in the Australian market. My three co-founders Adam McWhinney, Conrad Yiu and Mark Coulter also recognised this opportunity, and we got together over a few beers, sketched out a plan and decided to launch Temple & Webster.

Bernadette: What was the plan?

Brian: Step one was to fully map out how big the homewares and furnishing market was by category to see what the potential penetration from an online perspective would be. Step two was working out if we should target everyone or just a select demographic.

Bernadette: What research data did you use to scope out the market?

Brian: We looked at ABS data which showed that about 70 per cent of spend in the homewares and furnishing category came from the top 50 per cent of households by household income, so that pointed us in the right direction. We knew that if we were going to capture a large share of the market efficiently, then we would need to target this demographic.

Unique to Australia, but loosely resembling a US online retailer, www.onekingslane.com, Temple & Webster's cost-effective business model enabled them to be competitive at the outset. Brian explains:

We are an online shopping club, and each week we present our million-plus members with over 3000 curated homewares and furniture items. Unlike traditional retailers, we don't hold inventory at the time of sale. The way our model works is that we collaborate with wholesalers, emerging designers and artisan suppliers to source homeware and furniture products from around the world. We agree which items to present to our member base, the sale theme and the quantity of products they will reserve for us for the duration of the sale event, which typically lasts for just five to seven days.

After the sale period has ended, our suppliers send us the exact number of products that have been ordered by our members. Our model effectively de-risks buying as we're only buying items that our members have said they would like to purchase.

For Temple & Webster, getting started was strictly business.

A passion for shoes and her business partners' passion for profit saw Jodie Fox's Shoes of Prey (www.shoesofprey.com) come to life.

Jodie: I had always liked shoes, but I could never find exactly what I wanted and if I did, it was rarely in my size. While I was travelling in Asia, I found someone I could commission to make shoes I'd designed, so I had my shoes made, like the tailors who make suits and shirts exactly to size, and the girls in my friendship circle said, 'This is great! Can you make some shoes for me too?'

Bernadette: Did your business partners share the same passion for shoes?

Jodie: My business partners had been looking for a business idea to invest in for some time, and while we were lying on the beach one Christmas we got talking about my online shoe idea. They weren't passionate about shoes but they were seeking out a business opportunity and waiting for that one killer idea, and this is how the business came together. What they were seeking happened to match what I was doing at the time. It was very organic.

The perfect marriage of passion and profit.

You could say John Winning started Appliances Online (www .appliancesonline.com.au) to prove a point.

My family owned the whitegoods company Winning Appliances and my dad was the general manager at the time. I went to him with the idea and said, 'I think that we could sell the products that we have got in the warehouse online'. They all thought that wouldn't happen but my dad agreed to give me a go, thinking, 'I'll give him a go, and if that doesn't work then he'll get back to the family business'. I convinced them that the amount of investment was small enough to warrant them giving me a go to prove to me that it wouldn't work. Luckily it did work and here we are today.

Work out what problem you are solving

The best way to establish what your business model will be is to work out what problem you are solving, and for whom.

This is the single most important factor when establishing not just an online business, but any business.

The best news is that by simply asking this question, you can access a never-ending supply of unique, profitable and sustainable business ideas.

Are all the good ideas gone?

I've often heard people say, 'Awwww, all the good ideas are gone; all the big industry disruptors' ideas: YouTube, Facebook, Snapchat. There's nothing left!'

If you've ever thought that way, you'll love this section because you'll see that simply by changing the question, you can open up an entire world of brand-new business ideas.

Hoping to get in on the ground floor of whatever trend was about to take off, I asked numerous entrepreneurs the questions I really, really wanted their insight on. And they were:

- Where are the untapped niches?

- What products or services are yet to be created that you think will 'go off'?

- What global markets are about to explode in a frenzy of demand, and for what?

Turns out I'd been asking the wrong question all along. Mark Middo, author of the book *5 Minute Business* set me on the right path.

The question you really need to be asking is not 'What product is yet to be invented?' but 'What problem has yet to be solved?'

For example, when I saw people struggling to build an online business, I wrote my book *5 Minute Business*. It sold like hotcakes because it addressed a key need that a lot of entrepreneurs have, and that's how to get started quickly.

The light bulb came on. I got it. I was coming at it from the wrong angle. I had fallen into that age-old trap of thinking like a seller, not a marketer.

I had been asking the wrong question.

> The question you really need to be asking is not 'What product is yet to be invented?' but 'What problem has yet to be solved?'
>
> **Mark Middo**

By asking, 'What problem is yet to be solved?', the entire marketplace opens up. You stop thinking of products that need to be devised and sold ('push' marketing) and start thinking of creating products that help people get solutions to their unmet wants and needs ('pull' marketing).

By asking the right question, suddenly every unmet problem or need becomes a potential new business for you.

These ideas are being discussed all the time, not seriously, but in conversation, in passing. They are often prefaced with:

- 'I wish someone would... (insert unmet need)'.

- 'You know, they oughta... (insert unmet need)'.

Here's how some people have capitalised on this template:

- 'I wish someone would... create an app that captures a Snapchat picture so I can look at it later' (Snapkeep).

- You know, they oughta... make an app that tells us where the fish are swimming so we can catch more of them' (Fishfinder).

This concept is quite profound in its simplicity. Think of a problem you and your friends experience on a regular basis and see if you can come up with a solution – bingo! There's your new business idea, ready for testing.

And the best bit is, every new product created generates a whole series of other new problems that also need to be solved.

Who'd have thought Facebook would launch a generation of 18-year-old social-media strategists consulting to 58-year-old corporate titans who haven't got a clue what these kids do but just sign the cheque anyway and hope for the best.

Who'd have thought that Minecraft would spawn a raft of middle-aged, cardigan-wearing, geeky men making a fortune from AdSense with their YouTube clips teaching millions of eight-year-old boys how to build a quartz house from the Nether.

Ideas are inexhaustible because we'll always have problems that need solving. Not in the I-wish-my-husband-would-take-out-the-rubbish-without-me-asking type of problem, or the I-wish-he-wouldn't-wash-the-dishes-and-then-leave-that-one-unwashed-saucepan-in-the-sink sort of problem (that's another book).

> Often, it's a person who has worked in one job all their life who comes up with a brilliant invention.
>
> Paul Greenberg

But, you know, important problems: stuff-that-needs-to-get-done types of problems. We call it solving problems. Fancy types call it product innovation.

Paul Greenberg of Deals Direct knows a thing or two about innovation, having devised the concept of fixed-priced auctions for eBay all those years ago. He told me how that came about.

> I realised that although there was a lot of fun and excitement to be had with eBay auctions, I also knew that some people just wanted to buy the products then and there without mucking around with the auction process. So that's how we came up with 'fixed price'.

I was curious to see if Paul had a creative process for coming up with new product ideas or inventions.

Often, it's a person who has worked in one job all their life who comes up with a brilliant invention. They might work on a production line and see the same problem on the conveyor belt occurring day after day. They think to themselves, 'you know, if only someone would invent a bolt that stopped the conveyor belt doing that, then it would make this whole machine work better'. That's the kind of problem solving I'm talking about. Often an idea for a new product will come from a person who has a detailed knowledge about a particular occupation.

But of course, as is often the way, the people who have the idea often don't have the ability to bring it to market, which is why so many great ideas fail to manifest. A successful enterprise often requires both the inventor and a marketer and it's rare that someone has both skill sets. Not impossible, but rare.

The creation of a new product for a mining company is a case in point.

Cameron, a 35-year-old, hard-living man has been a mechanic all his adult life, working in remote locations around the country. In the heady days of the mining boom, he found himself in Western Australia, working in the mines, and was assigned to repairing the oversized tyres on the mining trucks.

'After a while of fixing these tyres, some of them as big as small houses, I noticed that the tools we were using weren't really cut out to do the job on tyres as big as this. So I got together with a tool guy and I showed him what I needed and he made it. I presented it to the boss and he went for it straight away as he could see that it would cut hours off the repair time just by using this customised tool built specifically for these tyres. That's what got me started. Now I manufacture the tool, export it all over the world and it's a very neat little business. Let's just say I don't have to work too hard these days.'

His specialised knowledge coupled with the toolmaker's design acumen enabled them to create a new product from scratch which fixed a niche problem that few outside their industry would know existed. But the market was big enough, and lucrative enough, to support the production of the tool...and the rest, as they say, is history.

So if you're looking for the 'next big thing' or the next 'killer app', it's best not to ask, as I did, 'How can I make money?' but to ask 'What problems need solving?'

Should you start with the end in mind?

Authors often say they don't start writing a book until they know what the ending is. Others jump in and work it out as they go.

I was curious to discover whether the entrepreneurs went into their businesses with an end in mind – to sell it, or go public – or whether it just grew organically, without a lot of planning.

Gabby Leibovich, co-founder of Catch of the Day (www.catchoftheday .com.au), certainly didn't have any grand plans when he started his business out of his garage in suburban Melbourne.

> All we had in mind when we launched was to have a job, make sure the kids got fed and pay rent. We started selling random stuff at the market — clothes, shoes, handbags — and then we started selling on eBay. We put on a team of six people and it literally happened one day at a time, bit by bit. People ask every day, 'Did you expect it to become as big as it is today?' and the honest truth is no. I still pinch myself every day not really realising how we got to where we are.

Today he employs more than 500 people and is on track to turn over one billion dollars.

Paul Greenberg had this to say about his business, which went public in early 2014.

> I didn't have a grand plan when I started, but that's just me. I was never a huge fan of the 'exit strategy' theory. Maybe I should have been, but my intuitive sense is that if you've got a good business, then anyone would want to buy it, and then you won't have a problem selling it. Ultimately, your focus should be on building a good business that's easy to run. And make it so that it doesn't just become your baby, unable to be run by anyone but you, and then you won't have any shortage of buyers.

What business are you in?

One of the most valuable lessons I learned working as an account director at the direct marketing advertising agency Wunderman Cato Johnson was that before you start work on any campaign, you must answer one important question, the answer to which informs everything else, and I mean *everything*.

And the question is (drum roll, please): *What business are you in?*

It sounds so simple, but the answer is often not what we think. Let me give you an example.

One of the agency's clients at the time was Kodak. This was the early 1990s and things weren't so bad for them at the time, but they weren't looking so good either.

At the time you could understand that when they were asked what business they were in, the logical answer was, 'We're in the film business'.

As the leader in film processing worldwide, they had the market sewn up, so as far as they were concerned, when we asked them who their competitors were, they said, 'We don't really have any'.

In hindsight, it's clear they were not in the film processing business at all, but instead, in the 'memory preservation' or the 'data capture' business. Just that slight, but ever so important, shift in focus changes everything. Does it matter? Yes … a lot.

Here's why.

Kodak considered themselves to be in the film processing business, ergo they had no real competition and ergo they didn't need to worry. Big mistake!

If they had considered themselves to be in the 'memory preservation' business, they would have considered themselves to have oodles of competition (data storage, USB technology, digital imaging and more recently cloud computing), ergo they would have been super vigilant about how they were going to protect their turf and ergo they would have been looking ahead to see what was coming. They had the technology but they fundamentally forgot what business they were in. (I'll stop using the word 'ergo' now. I know. It's very annoying.)

Kodak is pedalling furiously now to make up for those lost opportunities and are now capitalising on the deep technological expertise it has developed over the years in materials science, deposition and digital imaging science, a far cry from its core service offering back in the '90s.

We're all in the data business

So, knowing how important it is to get the answer to 'What business are you in?' right, I was curious to see what each entrepreneur said when I asked them that very same question. As expected, they were way ahead of the game.

'We are an analytics company that sells shoes.' *Gabby Leibovich, founder of Catch of the Day*

'We are a data company that sells creative services.' *Matt Barrie, co-founder of Freelancer*

'We are a logistics company that sells books.' *Tony Nash, co-founder of Booktopia*

'We are a data company that sells music.' *Jane Huxley, general manager of Pandora Australia and NZ*

'We are a logistics business that sells appliances.' *John Winning, founder of Appliances Online*

John Winning gets even more meta, if there's such a thing.

We are a logistics company that happens to sell appliances. We are a technology business that happens to sell appliances. We are a marketing and advertising agency that happens to sell appliances. Each area of the business needs to be the best at what it can be.

Of course, few of them started out thinking of themselves as data companies. They were obsessed with selling what they sold, but as the company grew – as the databases expanded, the customers increased, the product line-up multiplied – the need to keep track of what people were buying, when, where and how became so great they had to develop new and sophisticated reporting systems just to manage the data.

When they could see the revelatory insights that the data provided, they got more and more interested in seeing how they could apply those insights to making the business more efficient. They measured everything: Cost of acquisition; Basket size; Time on site; Average order sale; Bounce rates; Time of purchase; Coupon redemptions; Email open rate... the metrics just keep on coming.

Booktopia's Tony Nash says, 'We can predict who is expecting a baby in the next year based on the books they have bought'.

The entrepreneurs didn't say this, but to me it seemed as if the products they were selling were almost irrelevant to the business, just commodities to be moved from one point to another. It was the metrics and the insights they provided that became their focus.

Shoes of Prey creator Jodie Fox candidly admitted she took a while to join the dots.

> In hindsight, I would have been much more data-oriented earlier on. The boys were great at being data-oriented early on but it took me a little while to understand that and really bring that into my method of working.

I met an advertising recruitment consultant at an event a while back. I asked her, 'What are the hottest jobs at the moment?' With nary a pause, she answered, 'Data analysts. Can't keep up. Know any?'

According to Freelancer's Matt Barrie, somewhat cryptically, 'software is eating the world'.

> The biggest direct-marketing company in the world is a software company. It's Google. The fastest growing telecom company in the world is a software company. It's Scribe (which is Microsoft). And the biggest book seller, the biggest shoe seller and soon to be the

biggest retailer in the world is a software company. It's Amazon. Nearly every single industry is waking somewhat disruptively to discover it's a software business.

And of course, never before has access to data like this been so easy to find. Google Analytics, CRM systems like Salesforce and InfusionSoft and email management products like AWeber, ACT, MailChimp, Constant Contact and the like have delivered them an avalanche of data that they can now review with laser-like precision to know what the customer wants before they even know it themselves.

When distinctions like this are made and when you know what business you're in, you start doing things such as hiring differently.

Andre Eikmeier, co-founder of the online wine retailer Vinomofo (www.vinomofo.com), reflects on what he could have done starting out.

> It's really important to understand right from the get-go that as an online business we are as much an internet company as we are a wine company. So right from the start, what we would have done differently is invite a developer to be one of the founders, a tech guy. Ideally, for an online business, what you want is a hacker who can code and a hustler who can sell as part of your founding team. Otherwise, you're in the hands of agencies, which are expensive and not particularly productive, or you're in the hands of a young guy who's building the site but doesn't have real world experience and it just doesn't work.

> **Every online company needs a hacker and a hustler, preferably as founding partners.**
>
> **Andre Eikmeier**

Don't give up your day job—or should you?

So there's all the hard, big-picture thinking done.

You've worked out your vision and what you want: a lifestyle business or global domination?

You've worked out what you're selling and what problems you're solving.

You've chosen the passion or profit path (or, ideally, a bit of both) and now you know what business you're in. It's all happening!

So the next big question — and I get asked this a lot by start-up entrepreneurs, copywriting students, freelancers and those working full time but wanting to get started on something new — is, 'Should I give up my day job to pursue this full time? Or should I wait until it's more solid and just transition from full-time work to my own business as demand grows?'

Having been a jobbing actor, I would have starved had it not been for my back-up plan of a marketing and training business. Some would say you can't succeed precisely *because* you have a back-up plan, but I don't agree. I saw a famous Australian actor who was big in the 1990s behind the counter of a shop selling greeting cards at Darling Harbour in Sydney. I think he probably wished he'd had a back-up plan. Not that there's anything wrong with selling greeting cards of course! But I digress.

Opinions will vary on this one, and of course, everyone's personal circumstances and tolerance for risk will dictate different choices, but I recommend transitioning.

One of my copywriting students, Belinda Weaver, founder of the global copywriting business Copywrite Matters (www.copywritematters .com.au), reveals how she got her new business up and running while still working full time for her boss and then taking the business with her when she left — all with his approval!

> I started my copywriting business while working full time. My first few copywriting clients came through a referral agreement and then I started getting enquiries through my social media network and after six months I could see a consistent pipeline of work.
>
> That's when I decided to remove my safety net and go full time in my business. But rather than simply resigning, I explained to the managing director that I was leaving the business but that I

could still do the tasks that required my marketing expertise, like strategy and copywriting. I outlined that they wouldn't have to hire and train a new marketing resource. The work would be done and, even paying me my new contractor rate, they would still save tens of thousands of dollars each year. My first regular client was secure. It was a fantastic start to my business.

But my advice for hedging your bets and covering all bases while killing two birds with one stone (I'll stop mixing my metaphors now) could not be more different from Jodie Fox's advice on how to get an entrepreneurial venture started.

Bernadette: *Should entrepreneurs give up their day jobs to focus on their new endeavours?*

Jodie: We all have this funny dream when we start our business, which is, 'I will start the business and then when it is making enough money to pay my current salary I will slip over to that business'. And the fact of the matter is that this is just not how it works.

If you are just giving it a little bit of time on the side you are never going to turn it into a business that is going to pay your salary. You need to take a risk and step into it and see if you can make it happen, otherwise you run the risk of the business failing because you weren't there enough.

Bernadette: *How did you manage the transition?*

Jodie: For the early trips to visit suppliers I was still working in advertising and after about a year, I left my job in advertising to go full time into the business. I was very much doing two jobs and the hours were okay, but it was the mental energy, and the ability to slip between the two that was really challenging for me.

Jodie and her business partners had looked ahead, saving diligently for a couple of years prior to starting the business to tide them over those first few difficult years, so although they were by their own definition 'living on two-minute noodles', they weren't exactly starving and living in a garret.

Note: living in a garret is completely over-rated. And what the heck is a garret anyway? (Definition from Wikipedia: 'habitable attic or small – and possibly dismal or cramped – living space at the top of a house', just in case you're interested).

However, author of *5 Minute Business* Mark Middo fell firmly on the side of transitioning.

> People should not give up their day job until their side project has a real hold in the market. You've got to find a niche and ensure the niche is big enough to support what you're selling. The reality is that there is more opportunity now than ever with the web so there's lots of potential to do well. But it's worth testing your idea before giving up full-time work and a pay cheque, just in case the idea doesn't have traction.

Shaun O'Brien, managing director of Selby Acoustics (www.selby .com.au), a leading online retailer of electronic accessories and components, took the safe, but more exhausting, option.

> I just really worked my bum off! I was working full time as well, so I didn't need to create a business immediately, but for the first two years I reinvested all the profits into more stock, more product and building the business. That made it easier and it also made it harder because I was trying to juggle two things at once. But growth just continued and I was used to managing staff, so I put staff on as needed.

What to expect when you're expecting success

If you're expecting your online business journey to be smooth, forget it. For those who prefer life and business to unfold in a logical, orderly progression, this ain't the business for you kid. Scram! Geddouttahere!

> People should not give up their day job until their side project has a real hold in the market.
>
> **Mark Middo**

To be a successful online entrepreneur, there's one thing you'll have to get comfortable with, and that's uncertainty.

Challenges starting out

Without wanting to sound pessimistic, Murphy was right: creating an online business will take longer than you think, cost more than you think, be harder than you think and be less fun than you think.

And just as you get it to where you want it, you'll need to reinvent it because a competitor has moved in or the market's moved on and you've become out of date. Tough gig, online business.

For some reason, we often believe that those who are already successful have always been successful. That they never made a mistake, lost money, backed a dud, got it wrong—which is why it's always so refreshing to hear the hard-luck tales of our heroes. And I'm just the person to bring those stories to you, not because I'm one to indulge in schadenfreude (oh all right, maybe I am a bit), but because sometimes it's insightful and comforting to hear about the misfortunes of others; it helps us shake off our failures and mis-steps that little bit more easily, knowing that others before us have done the same.

> **Tip**
> To be a successful online entrepreneur, there's one thing you'll have to get comfortable with, and that's uncertainty.

Andre Eikmeier reflects on his early days creating the online wine retailer Vinomofo.

> We didn't have any capital. We started from scratch with nothing so we had to construct a model that would be cashflow positive. We knew that the revenue growth would have to fund the business before the profit kicked in. We also knew we couldn't afford to buy all the stock, so that was a challenge too. We struck a deal with the wineries and arranged that we would let them know every few days how many we wanted, so it was constructed on the fly. As it turns out those limitations worked for us and we constructed a model, a product and a message around those advantages.

Even seasoned operators with decades of experience like Stephanie Alexander are not immune to the challenges of transitioning to a digital world. Author of the famous cookbook *The Cook's Companion*, she reflected on the difficulty of bringing her massive cookbook to life as an app.

> The biggest challenge for us was the cost. I was investing the money in this project and I found it tricky when what was an original quote kept swelling to more and more and more. At a certain point in the project you really are committed and you can't back out of it when they say now it's going to cost an extra $12000. It's all linked. You can't go backwards. It's not good when the original quote has got nothing to do with what it finally costs. I don't like that.

Who gives a crap?

No, I'm not being belligerent. That's the name of Simon Griffiths' social enterprise, Who Gives a Crap, a toilet-paper production company that sends part-profits to the developing world to fund construction of sanitation services. But who in their right mind would enter into one of the most hotly contested categories in the fast-moving consumer goods market, going up against the likes of Procter & Gamble, Carter Holt Harvey and Unilever? Well, Simon did. And with zero budget, zero manufacturing experience and zero experience he is now carving out a niche that had heretofore been untapped, targeting people who care where their toilet paper comes from and where the proceeds go. Crappers with a conscience, shall we say?

So how on earth do you start something like this? With major competitors breathing down your neck, no distribution and no customers, the barriers to success were overwhelming. But, like most social activists with a good idea, he sat down for what he believed in, and the rest, as they say, is history.

> We had to think differently. We had to get the capital behind us to make the product, so we ran a crowdfunding campaign to pre-sell the first $50000 of toilet paper. And to help things along, I agreed to sit on a toilet, with a live web feed transmitted out to the world until we hit the target.

Yes, you read correctly. A live web feed. Simon did not get off that toilet until the final pledge was in, despite experiencing hallucinations from sleep-deprivation, aching muscles for sitting so long and a very sore bottom.

The video went viral and attracted worldwide media attention. And they reached their target. That's what I call commitment.

Shaun O'Brien of Selby Acoustics had similiar, but different challenges.

> My biggest challenge was I had zero capital. I started the business with $100, so I bought $100 worth of stock. And I have never invested any other money in it at all since then, so doing everything on a very tight budget was always tough. I had no experience online, my computer skills were almost zero and finding suppliers was incredibly difficult. In 2003 the internet was almost a dirty word as far as traditional retail was concerned and getting suppliers to stock us was near on impossible, so it was just persistence, but we worked with the suppliers gradually and as we showed success with one supplier another one would come on board.

* * *

So here's what we've covered so far.

You've thought about why you want an online business, or why you want to take your existing business online. Maybe it's to generate a bit of cash to pay for an overseas holiday every year or maybe it's because you'd like to buy a penthouse in Trump Tower. Getting clear on your 'why' is the starting point.

From there, you've worked out whether that goal will be best achieved by setting up a lifestyle business or a growth/equity business.

A lifestyle business is a business that is set up and run by its founders primarily with the aim of sustaining a particular level of income – no more or no less – or for providing a foundation from which to enjoy a particular lifestyle.

A growth business is all about making the big bucks, getting investors, getting listed and getting the accolades. Make no mistake, this is a lifestyle too. It's just a very extreme lifestyle that will have you following the business rather than the business following you.

Both are good and both can be desirable; it just depends on what you want.

You'll then want to decide on what you're selling: will you sell something that you're passionate about or do you just want to sell whatever people are buying? Either way, without a deep understanding of how to generate awareness and leads, it's going to be a tough road. Your passion for your topic might create the momentum you need to get you over the humps, but at some point, you'll need to get good at marketing.

Part of marketing, of course, is understanding your target market and working out its problems. If you can discover a problem that is yet to have a solution, and it's a problem experienced by a sizeable portion of the population, and they're prepared to – and can afford to – pay your price, you could be onto a winner. The key to finding a great business idea is not asking 'What markets are yet to be tapped?', but by asking 'What problems are yet to be solved?'

You'll then want to ask the bigger questions, like 'What business am I in?' so that you can discover who your real competitors are and be fully cognisant of the challenges you're about to face. Getting the answer to this wrong can be a major deal-breaker so don't assume the answer is obvious. It's often not. Who are you *really* competing with?

And then the practical questions arise, like 'Should I start slow and transition into my new business while I work full time and have the luxury of a regular pay cheque, or should I just jump in, boots 'n' all, and give it my best shot?' Both have merits, but both require planning so if you've got an idea for an online business, start thinking now – right now – about how you'll find the time to bring it to life, whether it will turn a profit straight away or whether you'll need to save up for a year or two or transition between full time work and your business while it finds its feet.

Knowledge is power, and knowing what you're up for before you start any new endeavour can often be the difference between success and failure.

What's next?

Read on to find out more about the people behind some of Australia's most successful businesses: which qualities they all have in common that guarantee their success; how they think; the lessons they've learned; how they've dealt with failure, stress or overwhelming stuff-ups; how they created their unique points of difference and got their businesses off the ground; and much more.

CHAPTER TWO
PEOPLE

No man will make a great leader who wants to
do it all himself or get all the credit for doing it.

Andrew Carnegie

What do all great online entrepreneurs have in common?

This chapter explores the people behind the business, and why they can bring an idea to life and turn it into a multimillion-dollar business while others, equally intelligent and equally capable, struggle to get an idea off the ground. What is it about these entrepreneurs that separates them from those who haven't succeeded?

We take a look at the personal philosophies that underpin their management strategies, their values and their personal mission statements on the way things should be done. We look at how they cope with stress, email overload, failure, setbacks and rejection, and how they keep on keeping on when everything feels like it's falling apart. I wanted to know what worries them, and how they deal with the 3 am terrors – when they wake wondering if they can really get up and go through it all again.

I wanted to know who and what inspires them, what they regret, and why and, if they had their time over, what they'd do differently.

'It's easy for them'

When outsiders look in on the lives of successful entrepreneurs and see them feted at award ceremonies, in the media or at gala events, the perception is often, 'Well, it's easy for them to succeed – they had contacts, money, experience, education'. But from my research, that's often not the case. We can sometimes rationalise others' success and our lack thereof by finding reasons why it was easy for them and hard(er) for us. With the exception of one or two, most of the people I interviewed started bootstrap businesses with nothing but an idea, a passion for success and a hunger to see their personal potential fulfilled. For many of them, it was not about what they could get, but about what they could *become* – and their business was the catalyst for that personal exploration.

They all worked hard, and still do, to bring their ideas to life. They burned the midnight oil, spent time away from partners and children, relocated to foreign countries, sacrificed short-term pleasures for long-term gains, and did the things they needed to do to make the business work. There were no shortcuts, fast-tracks or handouts here.

As you'll see, things didn't always work out for them as planned but, as they say in the movies, when you get lemons, you make lemonade.

The 5 personal qualities of all successful online entrepreneurs

After interviewing the entrepreneurs, it became clear that they all have a success mindset, a way of thinking, being and doing that enables them to:

1. Reframe failure: they see failure as feedback

2. Do what others don't, won't or can't: they push through their own personal barriers of resistance to do what needs to be done

3. Know their story and mission: they know what they do and can communicate it effortlessly

4. Delegate: they know that done is better than perfect and aren't afraid to cede control to others around them

5. Have depth of vision: they anticipate with accuracy what their business, and their clients, will need next.

If you want to create a successful business, you'll have a better chance of making it happen by embracing these five principles.

1. Reframe failure

You often hear of people saying that going broke, getting sued or getting sick was 'the best thing that ever happened to me'. I don't know about you, but when I hear that I just think they've become very good at rationalising what was an unpleasant experience, or that they've used positive-psychology techniques to create a level of acceptance that makes life easier to bear.

I'm not condemning the practice. I do it myself. I constantly reframe shite situations and events so that I can move on without feeling angst, bitterness or regret. It doesn't always work, but hey, it's better than feeling vengeful or murderous rage for those who have wronged us.

So I was interested to see that many of the entrepreneurs I interviewed used these same reframing techniques to not only minimise the emotional cost of failure, but to actually leverage those experiences to create better, more successful businesses than those they started with.

Accessorise!

If Shaun O'Brien, founder of Selby Acoustics, hadn't failed at his first business, there's no way he would have succeeded at his second. Like many in the early 2000s, Shaun was attracted to the high margins that could be made selling TVs and other big-box electronic items online direct to the customer. But what he didn't bank on was the plethora of hassles and hurdles that came with eliminating the middleman.

I didn't realise until I got into it that firstly, it's really expensive to repair electronics like TV and audio systems. They are enormously intricate, require stocking of lots of different parts and require quite high levels of skill to fix. Add to that the high costs of shipping bulky goods to and from the customer across Australia and the fact that servicing the customer can be very time-consuming, and I discovered very early on that all that glitters is definitely not gold when it comes to selling electronics online.

> I discovered very early on that all that glitters is definitely not gold when it comes to selling electronics online.
>
> Shaun O'Brien

But fortunately, what he also discovered was that the accessories that people needed to make their electronics work – the cables, the wall mounts, the nuts and bolts, the brackets – were everything electronics wasn't.

I could see pretty quickly that the accessories were smaller so they were easier and cheaper to ship, had fewer moving parts so they had fewer technical problems and therefore required little or no servicing, and I realised after lots of sleepless nights, that maybe I should be selling accessories instead of electronics.

So, that's how Selby Acoustics got started. Like the phoenix rising, his second business grew from the failure of his first.

What's in a name?

Andre Eikmeier loved wine. He loved it so much that he and his brother-in-law created Quaff, an online wine community, to discuss their love of it and share their thoughts and wisdom with other like-minded wine lovers – things like which wine they drank, why they liked it, why they didn't, what food it went with, how much it cost, was it good value, what was better value, and so on. Their primary aim was to sell monthly memberships to the club so that people could get high-quality information about wine 'without all the bowties and bulls**t' from people who knew about wine but had no vested interest in pushing any particular product. However, after four hard years slogging it out they had to come to terms with the painful realisation that, in Andre's own words, 'Nobody wanted to pay for what we were offering'.

The business had failed. Or had it? Although they hadn't sold many memberships, what they did have was an engaged community. As the primary breadwinner with two children in private schools to support, and four years invested in the business, Andre – along with his brother-in-law – had to make a decision. Should they just walk away from what they had built or give it one more shot? What that 'shot' was they weren't too sure, but they knew they had a passionate community of wine lovers.

'We said to ourselves, instead of just recommending wine, why don't we sell it too!' Andre says.

Their decision was vindicated when, within just a week of launching their first product, they were inundated with sales. Andre says, with a wry smile:

> Our success was largely due to the Quaff community we had built up over those first four years. They were our first customers. It was as if they were saying, 'You've been telling us what to buy for four years—it's about time you sold us something!' To be honest, we felt pretty stupid that we hadn't cottoned onto that more quickly.

But the road to success was not smooth. Three days prior to the launch of their new business, they received a letter that changed everything.

> We were going to launch this cool wine site called Vinomojo, and we were all set to go. We got the first web pages up, the Twitter pages were ready, and we had a teaser campaign set to go. But three days out from launching we got a 'cease and desist' letter from a public company that owned a wine brand called Mojo wines saying we couldn't proceed using that name or we'd be subject to legal action. But at the same time, we couldn't stop as we'd come this far.

They could have called it a day, thrown their hands in the air and declared it all too hard. But they didn't. Here's what they did.

> We got together that night for an emergency meeting—which may have involved a little bit of alcohol—and to be honest, we were a bit stressed, but we just started throwing ideas around and after about three hours of coming up with nothing, my business partner Justin says, 'Let's just call it Vinomofo for the motherf*****s who are trying to stop us from launching!'

Laughing at the memory, Andre was quick to add, 'It wasn't funny at all back then though'.

> My business partner Justin says, 'Let's just call it Vinomofo for the motherf*****s who are trying to stop us from launching!'
>
> Andre Eikmeier

And the rest, as they say, is history. They launched the business and their distinctive, slightly risqué name has become one of their most valuable branding assets. When you get lemons...

When right beats might

Imagine the tension 23-year-old Daniel Flynn experienced from well-meaning family and friends when he decided to forgo a promising career in property development and put aside his recently completed university degree to start selling bottled water to help raise funds to support projects in the developing world. 'Mmm, pass the salt please, Daniel', you can hear his mum say, voice tight with disapproval.

You can understand their concern. From their perspective, the picture looked grim: he was going head to head against Coke, the world's biggest soft-drink maker, with no budget, no experience, no team, no distribution—and to cap it off, he wasn't even going to take a salary until the business could pay its way. The road to success for Daniel was as potholed as a Cambodian cow track. The blows kept coming.

> We had a lot of trouble getting started. It was as if we were jinxed. Nothing went right. Within a week of receiving our first order for 50000 bottles we had to do a national product recall as the labels got scrunched when they were printed onto the bottles. The labels

are a big deal for us because they contain a tracking code, which is how the consumer can track the profit from that bottle to the project it supports. We dealt with that, but six months after that happened, our first supplier didn't supply any products for five weeks, so we lost 350 of our stockists, which was about 90 per cent of our business. All that work we'd put into building up our distribution channel had just disintegrated overnight. It took a lot of time to build back that trust, but we persisted.

But wait, there's more...

We got a new distributor on board and they promised us big numbers, but within a month of launching with them, they went into liquidation. And then, after 11 months negotiating with a major supermarket to get national ranging, the very next week a new category manager took over and ousted us because he didn't think our product was any good. We couldn't take a trick. It was a nightmare.

Like justice, the wheels of progress for Daniel turned slowly.

It was a pretty miserable three years. In year one we made a profit of $7500, which went to our first project, in year two it was $7800, in year three it was $20000.

But when success arrived, it was sweet.

People started to get us. They realised that they could buy water from a large multinational and not get any benefit other than a bottle of water. Or they could buy it from us, still get the water and see that the profit from the purchase could help make another person's life better. It's a no-brainer really. Six years in, we have raised over $1.8 million for projects—and it's growing exponentially.

You can see that Daniel's 'why'—his purpose for being in business—was stronger than any setback he could possibly experience and that his drive to make a difference was what kept him going.

It's a really cool thought that when I wake up in the morning I know that what I've done the day before and what I'm going to do that day actually changes people's lives. What they say is true: 'Choose a job you love and you will never have to work a day in your life'. That's how I feel.

A little site called eBay

For some people, a burning passion to help others is the foundation of their 'why' and the reason they do what they do. For Paul Greenberg, his burning passion was to remove himself and his wife from the stress, pressure and constant danger of living in one of the most violent countries on the planet, South Africa. Unable to transfer the wealth he had at the time due to government currency restrictions and unfavourable exchange rates, he had to get creative.

> We were only allowed to take the equivalent of $20000 with us to Australia, which is not a lot when you're starting from scratch, and a few personal effects. Fortunately, I was allowed to take my vintage guitars with me, which was a decision that changed my life. When I got to Australia, and I have to say times were a little tough, a friend told me about a little site called eBay, so after getting online and seeing the potential, I put my guitars up for sale and couldn't believe how much people paid for them! It got me thinking: what else could I sell on eBay?

> I put my guitars up for sale and couldn't believe how much people paid for them! It got me thinking: what else could I sell on eBay?
>
> **Paul Greenberg**

That small decision to sell a few guitars led him to co-create Australia's first online department store, Deals Direct, which subsequently gave rise to the 'fixed price' function that is now a staple on eBay and other auction sites. Deals Direct went public in 2014 and Paul retired to become the executive chairman of industry group NORA (National Online Retailers Association).

From little things big things grow. For both Paul and eBay.

2. Do what others don't, won't or can't

One of my coaching clients, Jason, works as a senior manager with an importing company. Secretly, he'd love to chuck it in, set up an online business, work from home and be done with the commute, the office politics and everything else that goes with corporate life. He's got lots of business plans, ideas and aspirations, but can't get them off the ground. So I decided to find out why.

Bernadette: You talk about your app idea a lot, Jason. Just out of interest, how come you haven't done anything about it?

Jason: I don't have time!

Bernadette: Yeah, I know. Life is frantic. What did you get up to last weekend?

Jason: Saturday was our annual golf tournament for the footy club. We had an early start and it went for most of the day.

Bernadette: And what about Sunday?

Jason: I did a bike ride with my mates down Beach Road to the peninsula. Tough ride, but I have a tri coming up and need to keep fit.

Bernadette: And how long did that take?

Jason: About four hours and then I had coffee at the end to catch up with the boys.

Bernadette: And what did you do last night?

Jason: Well, it was cold, and I'd had a big week, so I just ordered a pizza, shared a bottle of red with my wife and watched a DVD with the kids.

Bernadette: So, no time to work on the app, hey? (said jokingly)

Jason: I had a busy week. Surely I'm entitled to a night off to relax? (said defensively)

I shared this story with one of the entrepreneurs and she replied, 'When I started building my business, a very wise mentor of mine said, "You can have results or you can have excuses, but you can't have both"'.

As you can see, what Jason excels at is excuses. We all do. Procrastination and rationalisation are the biggest reasons why we never accomplish anything of value in our lives. We're too busy waiting for the perfect moment to make that phone call, send that email, build that website, write that blog. We wait for inspiration to strike, which, like my desire to exercise, mostly never happens.

This resistance to taking action shows up in all sorts of interesting ways, often couched in 'Why should I?' negative self-talk like:

- *'Why should I* have to give up my Friday night to write a stupid blog when everyone else is watching *Game of Thrones*?'

- *'Why should I* have to forsake card nights with the boys to research shopping carts?'

- *'Why should I* have to stay up late to learn WordPress when everyone else is sleeping?'

Unsurprisingly, the entrepreneurs I interviewed excel at doing the things that others don't, won't or can't do.

As you'll discover from the following stories, successful entrepreneurs forsake a lot to build their businesses and they're not afraid to get their hands dirty either. There's not a lot of 'Why should I...?' going on with them.

Jump on a plane

When Dean Ramler and his mate and co-founder Ruslan Kogan hatched their plan to launch their online furniture site Milan Direct (www.milandirect.com.au), they didn't just go home to think about it, they bought a plane ticket to China.

> The day after we got the idea to sell designer furniture online, we researched 150 Chinese factories that could do what we wanted. We got the list down to a group of 20 and then we jumped on a plane to China and stayed there for weeks and weeks meeting all the factory owners, choosing the right suppliers, making sure that the people we eventually partnered with were able to deliver the quality we needed. We chose 12 factories, all of which we still use today.

Tip

Be hands-on. If you want to source a product from China, get on a plane and go to China.

Dean and Ruslan would have been quite within their rights to say, 'Why should we have to schlepp all over China, eat bad food and breathe bad air just to get this business off the ground?'

But that's not the way successful entrepreneurs think.

It's certainly not the way Jodie Fox and her two business partners thought when they pursued their vertical integration strategy and rented a factory in China to house their burgeoning bespoke shoe-making business.

Jodie: Between the three of us we take turns living in China supervising our new factory. It is of critical importance to be there to make sure that things are continuing to operate well, to see the opportunities, to push things along.

Bernadette: But couldn't you just hire someone in China to do that for you?

Jodie: There is a real barrier to getting things done when they know you're in another country. It's like, 'Oh you are not here so it doesn't really matter if we do it like this'. But the person who is going to turn up and say, 'Hey that is my order and I'd like it done like this!' – that's the person they are going to look after. Turning up in person is so important.

For Jodie, the sacrifices started long before the business even began.

I saved for two years prior to leaving The Campaign Palace (advertising agency) because I knew that the early days of the business were going to be tough and I wanted to have enough cash behind me to enable me to focus exclusively on the business for at least a couple of years.

Jodie could have spent her savings buying fancy shoes, but now, due to the hard work and sacrifice she put in a few years earlier, not only has she built a major asset that's making headlines around the world, but she can have however many shoes she wants. Better still, they all fit perfectly!

Get up early

Salvatore Malatesta, founder of the St. Ali group of cafes, the Sensory Lab in David Jones, and a social media marketing firm, is Melbourne's undisputed king of coffee. He is famous for having the foresight to see where the coffee industry was going, and he subsequently became the pioneer of coffee education and traceability, or 'provenance of the bean' if you like.

I was a dedicated customer of his sushi and coffee café at the University of Melbourne. The queues were 30-people deep because his coffee was so good and his sushi so fresh. I saw him open up the doors very, very early one morning, bleary-eyed. 'How are you?' I asked. 'Over it!' he said. 'These early mornings are killing me! With a baby at home, up half the night, I don't think I can take too many more [mornings]. I've never been a morning person either so this is doubly hard to take.' This was before he became an industry figure and he can now be more selective of the hours he works. But anyone who saw the hours he put in when building up his earlier businesses would be in no doubt that there is little glamour in building an empire, and that sometimes doing the very thing you hate is what you have to do to make it happen.

Stay relevant

I've travelled extensively with my elderly mother on group package tours through Europe, and my research shows that a high proportion of 70-year-olds play bridge, attend movie mornings or babysit grandkids. So you can understand why Stephanie Alexander, after a lifetime of cooking and writing recipe books, would have been well within her rights to start slowing down. But no, on the contrary, she's ramping up to create one of the most extensive apps an Australian chef has ever created. She'd already authored one of Australia's most popular and revered cookbooks, *The Cook's Companion*, but she didn't want to miss the opportunity of sharing her recipes with an entirely new generation of chefs.

It seemed like a good idea at the time to try and engage with the younger audience, who are definitely looking for recipes and product information in different ways from their parents. My audience has been using the book for 20 years and I wanted them to be able to say to their kids, 'This is a wonderful book and I use it all the time,' and for their kids to say, 'Yeah, we've got it on our phones and we can find almost anything we want really quickly'.

Did Stephanie have to build an app? No. But she knew that staying relevant was important so she did what she needed to do, irrespective of how costly or difficult the project may be.

Choose life!

As you start building your business, or take steps towards making your existing business more successful, it's worth noting some of the behaviours that successful entrepreneurs exhibit, to see if you can incorporate them into your way of living. Table 2.1 shows just a few of them.

Table 2.1: behaviours, qualities and traits of successful entrepreneurs

Unsuccessful entrepreneurs choose:	Successful entrepreneurs choose:
Comfort	Challenges
Safety	Growth
Invisibility	Visibility
Passive communication	Difficult conversations
Deferred decision-making	Fast decision-making

It may look easy from the outside, but often being successful means doing things you really, really don't want to do and experiencing emotions that you really, really don't want to feel. Those who 'feel the fear and do it anyway' are those who achieve success. Who said being a success was easy?

Go the extra mile

It's tempting to think that the qualities needed to succeed now as an entrepreneur are different from what they were 15 or 20 years ago. But I don't think they are. I think entrepreneurial qualities are evergreen irrespective of what advances in technology have been made or what the nature of the business is. Entrepreneurs will always display certain unique qualities.

Having worked for the legendary Harry M. Miller in the 1990s, I can say quite categorically that the qualities he showed then are over-represented in the entrepreneurs I interviewed. When they need to make something happen, they make it happen.

One of the many services Harry offered was brokering deals for people who were targeted by the media for one reason or another and who were unable or unwilling to manage the brouhaha that came with it. It was known as 'cheque-book journalism'. Harry's ability to find a story, sell it to a media outlet and take his cut along the way was well known. As this story demonstrates, he did what most wouldn't or couldn't.

Here's a situation I recall very well that gives some insight into his nose for news.

One of my jobs was to take phone calls from the public. People often rang us to report a news tip, reveal salacious gossip or seek media representation. My job was to determine the veracity of the call and filter out the nut jobs trying to get their 15 minutes of fame ('I know where the Beaumont kids are buried', 'I was probed by an alien who looked like Bob Hawke', 'I was part of a satanic ritual conducted by senior politicians at Parliament House', and the like).

It sounds easy to do, but without the internet, email and other research tools we take for granted today, trying to work out who was for real and who wasn't was really tough.

But I'll never forget the phone call that came in telling us there was a man in north Queensland who was living in a commune with, and supposedly married to, 13 women with 41 kids between them.

My nose for news had not been honed at this early stage of my career so I took the story to Harry, never sure which way he would jump. Stories I thought were good were met with, 'He's a crackpot. Move on'. Other stories, like this one, had him sitting bolt upright.

'Let me speak to them,' he said. After a flurry of phone calls to check and double-check that the story was based on fact, he barked, 'Hire me a private plane. We're going up there tomorrow'.

So, there we are, Harry and I, on a private plane flying into Queensland to meet this polygamist, his wives and an army of children. The story was indeed true and after much negotiation with the media, the story eventually ran on *60 Minutes* and in *Women's Weekly*, and was syndicated to newspapers around the country. It made Harry and the polygamist a lot of money.

The lesson to be learned here is that when an entrepreneur sniffs out an opportunity, they don't seek the womb-like comfort of a DVD, a glass of red wine and a pizza on a Friday night, nor do they mind giving up a card night, a golf day or an evening of *Game of Thrones*. No, they fly off in a tiny four-seater plane into the hinterland of Queensland to interview a polygamist. Or visit 20 factories in southwest China, trying to find a factory owner who speaks English. Or they sit on a toilet in a drafty warehouse trying to stay awake for 40 hours on live webcam to raise $50000 to make some toilet paper.

> **Tip**
>
> Do what others don't, won't or can't.

Entrepreneurs do things differently. They do what needs to be done.

3. Know your story and mission
'What do you do?'

We've all been asked it. We all ask it. At networking events, conferences, dinner parties and meetings across the world, the oft-asked question, 'What do you do?' is without doubt the ice-breaker of choice.

And for some entrepreneurs with a vast constellation of projects on the boil, it's a confusing one, with the answer changing depending on who they happen to be speaking to. Here's what happens to those who have too many ideas and not enough clarity when they get asked 'what do you do?'

'Hi, my name's Katie. Yeah, no. I...er...do a bit of this, a bit of that. Keep out of trouble, y'know.'

This impressive opening is then rounded off with a chortle and the inevitable boom-boom punchline: 'But enough about me, what do you think of me?', followed with the chaser that deflects any further scrutiny from taking place, 'No, seriously, what do *you* do?'

How many opportunities have been lost because we haven't got our elevator pitch right? I speak from experience. Having had a 'portfolio' career (a nice way of saying 'I've had a lot of jobs!'), I can tell you that sometimes I just can't be bothered even saying anything because it's just too darn complicated.

Honing the pitch

Like synchronised swimming, coming up with the 'elevator-pitch' is harder than it looks. So what's so hard about coming up with a 30-second statement?

Because distilling everything you do into one or two sentences presumes that you've answered a whole series of other higher order questions such as: What do you sell? Who to? For how much? Why do they buy from you? How are you different? What do you stand for?...and a lot more besides.

The art of refining your pitch is called 'knowing your story' and without it, it's practically impossible to position yourself in the market, get traction in the media or create a community.

That's why I found it interesting to see that, without exception, every entrepreneur I interviewed had their 'story' down pat (see table 2.2). Rehearsed. Seamless.

Table 2.2: entrepreneurs and their pitches

Entrepreneur	Pitch
Jodie Fox	Your perfect shoes
Brian Shanahan	Beautiful items for the home, beautifully priced
Dean Ramler	Designer furniture at great prices
Andre Eikmeier	Good wines, real people and epic deals, without all the bowties and bulls**t

Mission impossible

Having conducted dozens of management training programs for companies both big and small, I've seen first-hand the effort, time and money leaders put into creating a mission statement they hope will take them into their next phase of growth.

So why is it then, that after spending days in a windowless training room nutting out exactly how they want to be seen and why, the resulting one-page mission statement ends up on the foyer wall in a two-dollar photo frame from The Reject Shop, placed thematically next to the dusty 'Success' poster and is never looked at, referred to or commented on ever again?

For many companies, creating a mission statement was a workshop 'you had to have', a 'good thing to do', but mostly a waste of time that achieved very little except to fund the facilitator's annual holiday to Noosa. (Thank you, by the way.)

But now, it's different. Much different. In today's fast-paced, hyper-connected world, where start-up staff numbers can ramp up from 2 to 20 to 200 in the blink of an eye and where international offices in three different countries can be fitted out and staffed within weeks, *not* having a mission and clear sense of company values means things can, and do, go horribly awry.

Don't kill the dog

Take the story of a courier company delivering a curtain rod for their client. Their mission would appear to be 'Deliver on time at any cost'. We can't be sure what it was, but what we do know is that as the home owner wasn't home, the courier slipped the curtain rod through the letterbox and in through the front door. The homeowners returned home to find their dog pinned to the wall. True story.

Singing from the same song sheet

John Winning, founder of Appliances Online, knows a thing or two about mission and values. He has to. With more than 500 staff dotted around the country, keeping an eye on everyone is just not possible.

John: Having a clear mission is essential if you want to grow and retain the same values and have everyone working the same way. If we didn't have that we would have people all over the shop, not knowing what their role is. We would have to be pretty strict and have hands-on managers overseeing all the staff and telling them how to do their jobs.

Bernadette: How does that help staff make a decision?

John: It helps them understand what the belief, aims and missions of the company are, and then you give them the guidelines for the values and how they can act, and then allow them to go and do their job.

Bernadette: What are your company values?

John: Our 'rules' are our company values. And they are things like 'Impress Every Customer', 'Own Your Role' and 'One In All In'.

Our mission is to provide the best shopping experience in the world, so those are the things that help us make the decisions that we need to make. So if there's a job to be done, everyone pitches in and does it. If there is anything that needs doing for the customer, you make sure that they have the best experience in the world. These values and mission set the standards for how our delivery guys should act.

Bernadette: How does everyone know what the rules are?

John: They are publicly available.

(I can attest, having visited the Melbourne office, they are indeed pasted randomly all over various walls. Interestingly, they are not put in two-dollar photo frames, or even laminated. They're just printed up on 80 gsm paper and stuck on the wall with sticky tape. They look very much like 'working documents', visual reminders to help keep staff in touch with what they should always be thinking about.)

Bernadette: What about your customers? Do you show it to them?

John: We do, because we want them to know that we are accountable for this level of service. We want the customers to look at it and say,

'Well, you claim you are going to do this, then why don't you do it?' We have a video of the values on our website. That is not something we hide. We are quite happy to be held accountable to it.

When Shoes of Prey's Jodie Fox and her team of three outgrew the one-bedroom apartment they'd started in, she knew things had to change.

When we had a team of 15 people we realised that our culture and values had to be written down. We were all operating on what we thought were the right culture and values, but they were all slightly different to each other so we were making slightly different decisions, and people naturally have friction because of that. So now we have culture and values slides that are publicly available.

Tip

Whether you call it a mission statement, values or 'The Rules', make clear decisions on how you want people to treat each other. Write down the rules/values and plaster them all over the walls. And get staff to read them every day.

And they are. On SlideShare.

For these entrepreneurs, everything starts with the vision of the company. It's an active, living entity that informs their every decision.

4. Know how to delegate

Many entrepreneurs who've built their business from scratch and can do everything better than just about everybody else find it hard to let go, which makes it difficult for others, especially their employees, to get on with their job.

Conversations like this one can be heard across the nation.

Location: The pub
Day: Friday
Time: 6:47 pm
Present: Sam, Steve, Miranda

Scene 1

Sam: The boss is a bottleneck. If it wasn't for him, I could actually do my job.

Steve: I know. I get more done when he's out of the office than when he's in.

Miranda: He micromanages everything I do. While he fiddles, Rome burns.

Such conversations are commonplace: the classic scenario of the boss who can't let go.

So what happens when a business goes from zero to hero in months, not years? How does a boss retain control while giving their team the responsibility they need to make important decisions? After all, they can do every job that needs doing better than any of their employees, right? But does that mean they should be doing it?

Tony Nash from Booktopia started out doing everything: answering the phones, picking and packing, schlepping packages to the post office. He knew every job backwards. But as the company grew to 100 staff and four million titles on the website, he knew he had to delegate.

I had to ask myself, 'Can I do the task better than my employee?' And the answer is 'probably yes'. But only by 20 per cent and having a job done 20 per cent less well than me was a price I was willing to pay. Will they make mistakes? Yes, of course, but that's part and parcel of delegating and you have to accept that, but I'm happy to run with those odds if it means I can get work of higher value completed. It's in everyone's best interests that I put my attention on the things that make a real and measurable difference to the business.

With Booktopia turning over a whopping $40 million per year, I was curious to discover that Tony had only recently employed an executive assistant. Why did it take so long?

'I really don't know,' he says, with a smile. 'But it's been one of the best decisions I ever made.'

Hire well

When I visited Gabby Leibovich, founder of Catch of the Day, we took a stroll around his multistorey office, bypassing the oversized, colourful slippery-dip taking pride of place in the foyer. 'Does it ever get used?' I asked. 'Not much,' he replied.

What I found most interesting, however, was that few, if any, of the employees took much notice of him. They were too engrossed in their work. Some didn't even seem to *know* him. I don't think that's actually the fact; I just think his presence didn't faze them one little bit and there were certainly no 'quick-the-boss-is-in-the-house-look-busy!' shenanigans going on.

I look back on my time working with Harry M. Miller. We definitely knew when Harry was in the office. For a start, the Chinese whispers of 'he's coming, he's coming' would begin the minute he left the shabby-chic multistorey renovated factory/warehouse he called home, just 100 metres up the street from our office. His footsteps up the stairs kick-started a flurry as everyone rushed to their desks, keen to be 'seen' working.

He'd throw open the door and stand there like a sergeant major, waving a coffee mug in the air, yelling, '*Who left this dirty coffee cup in the sink?*' We'd all slink down in our chairs, hoping someone else would own up to the crime. I think he did it just for effect, just to make sure everyone knew who was in charge (as if there was any doubt).

Those were the days when output was measured by time spent in the office. Now, measuring performance is much easier and with an online business there are so many productivity and measurement tools that your boss can tell you not just how long you were online for, but what you searched for, what you bought and when. Include the fact that the average 20-year-old knows more about social media and technology than most 45-year-olds and the entire management paradigm has been completely subverted. That's why Gabby Leibovich had this to say about hiring:

> We hire for attitude. We have no C-level titles in our company. No CEO, no CFO, no CTO. And it works. When I went to the World Cup for six weeks, I barely got a phone call. That's my idea of how to run a business.

Matt Barrie of Freelancer was clear about what he looks for in new hires.

> Don't compromise on the people you hire. Make sure the team is always A-grade because A-grade people attract other A-grade people. B-grade people will attract C-grade people. You can't control all the business because it now runs 24/7, so you need really good people around to delegate to. Otherwise, you won't see success.

Brian Shanahan from Temple & Webster takes hiring seriously too.

> One thing that we deliberately don't do quickly is recruitment – indeed, candidates often have four or five interview rounds with different people across the team so we can get a sense of what the candidate is like, what drives them and whether they are the right cultural fit with our team. The time invested in finding the right people pays off, and today we have about 60 smart and passionate employees that love what they do.

Manage time efficiently

Most entrepreneurs are great at juggling multiple roles, businesses and responsibilities. I was keen to learn the secrets to multitasking.

When I went to the World Cup for six weeks, I barely got a phone call. That's my idea of how to run a business.

Gabby Leibovich

Darren Rowse, author of ProBlogger, is still heavily immersed in the full catastrophe of family life — and loving it. With three young boys, a wife working part-time and a number of businesses on the go, he must have some tips on time management.

Darren: It's about boundaries. It's about identifying the key things that have to be done in both areas of my life and then putting time aside and being protective about that time. As a blogger I have to set aside that time to writing and having a family. I have to be strict as to when that is, and everyone knows those times.

Bernadette: *Any tips on how to manage working from home?*

Darren: It's little things. My boys know that when my office door is open, they can come in for a chat. When the door is closed, they know not to interrupt.

Bernadette: *Social media can be very distracting too. Is that the case for you?*

Darren: I set aside a little bit of time every day for social media and that's it. I don't look into it unless I have absolutely nothing else on. I use automation and schedule posts ahead of time, but you want to be a bit careful about that because you want to be also engaging with people when they're online. We schedule posts at 6 am every morning and my audience expects it then, but I am not sitting there hitting 'Publish' on that post at 6 am. I just do it the night before and schedule it to go up in the morning.

> My boys know that when my office door is open, they can come in for a chat. When the door is closed, they know not to interrupt.
>
> Darren Rowse

Matt Barrie is to the point.

> Make sure you're busy for the right reasons! You've got to work smarter, not harder. It's good to be busy, but just make sure you're focusing on the right things and you're not being busy for the sake of being busy.

The Revenue Generator Form is a helpful template I see being used by lots of people. It has written at the top of it:

My top 3 revenue-generating activities for today are:

1. _____

2. _____

3. _____

This focuses the mind and ensures that if nothing but those three tasks are done, then the day has been a success. Life can get in the way of even the most important tasks, so by knocking off the profit-generating jobs first—often the most difficult—you can unleash a powerhouse of positive energy that will help you feel good about yourself for the rest of the day.

Email schmemail

Jodie Fox saves time in the morning by eating breakfast while conducting 'triage' on her emails.

> I try and get my emails to zero every day. That doesn't always happen, but you just can't have hundreds of emails sitting in your inbox because it is a mental drag that just sits with you and you will let people down. If there is something that I have to take action on, I will do it straight away and just email back and it's done. If I can't do it straight away then I will turn it into a Calendar item and it gets scheduled in my diary as an event.

Stephanie Alexander makes no bones about her work habits.

> I think I spend far too much time getting rid of useless emails that clog the system because I am so anal I can't stand looking at my inbox and having 50 emails that have just grown overnight. I have to get rid of them so I find that's taking half an hour of my day. I'm a bit of a workaholic so I tend to work seven days a week. My days are pretty structured and my personal assistant is here three days a week and we always have a lot to do on those three days. And of

course I have got two children and I like to see them too. So I just get on with it.

Simon Griffiths from Who Gives a Crap, thinks completely differently about efficiency.

I constantly have over a thousand unread emails in my inbox and it's just a matter of prioritising things. If something's not going to drive revenue it's not a priority. And you just accept that you're never going to be at that point where you have zero emails because that's when you're really inefficient.

5. Have depth of vision

As a self-confessed, dyed-in-the-wool, people-pleasing Aquarian, I find any level of disharmony, personal or professional, difficult to deal with, which is perhaps why I find criticism so gut-wrenching. I read the feedback forms evaluating a speech I've just delivered and routinely ignore the 20 forms that give me a glowing 9- or 10-out-of-10 rating, but hone in with laser-like intensity on the one that gave me a 6.

If you can't stand the heat...

As it turns out, you don't have to be a people-pleasing Aquarian to be sensitive to criticism. The entrepreneurs I interviewed have all been subject to much criticism, some of it vitriolic, and while it stings, they continue to function quite happily. The difference is that they've developed coping mechanisms that enable them to reframe the criticism into something more useful.

Stephanie Alexander refreshingly candidly says:

I find it as hard as anybody else to deal with criticism. I work through it. In the restaurant game we used to have the Rule of Three: it will hurt Day One; Day Two you'll still feel a twinge, but you'll have forgotten about it by Day Three. That always helped me through bad reviews or grumpy customers.

Simon Griffiths is equally forthright.

There's been a lot of sceptics who've come along and said, 'this will never work'. And there's definitely days where we still think that ourselves. So everything for us is really an experiment, but I think when you're faced with that style of criticism you've either got to use it as feedback to inform what you're doing as a business, or you need to really relish it and use that as a motivation to prove someone wrong, and that's how we dealt with it.

It's one thing for entrepreneurs to say they deal with criticism with great equanimity, but what do they really feel and do when they come face to face with a blistering attack on their business? I had the rare opportunity to witness it.

During my interview with Dean Ramler, I had Milan Direct's Facebook page open on my shared screen and as we were talking a complaint popped up in the feed. It was not pretty. I couldn't help but notice it and neither could he. I was torn. I was desperate to ask him, 'How does that make you feel – right here, in real time – this very pointed remark about your business?' but out of respect and courtesy, I didn't want to draw attention to it.

But then my curiosity got the better of me. I had to know.

Bernadette: Dean, you're probably reading that comment right there. I'm curious to know how that makes you feel. Does it upset you?'

Dean: Of course it does, and after this call I will look into what happened, but I think it's important that we never shy away from the fact you're not going to make 100 per cent of your customers happy. We have over 300 000 customers so it's inevitable that something is going to go wrong every now and then, but it's how we fix it that really matters.

Bernadette: You weren't tempted to pull the comment down?

Dean: You've got to take the good with the bad. We use these comments as an opportunity to reply to the customers and show the rest of the community that we back ourselves with our customer service and products. I view an upset customer as the biggest opportunity to turn him into a raving fan.

Bernadette: So how do you do that?

Dean: With most customers who are really annoyed, their expectation of your company is so low that when you go and provide them with good customer service you turn them from a really upset customer to a really happy customer. If you deleted the comment, then that implies you have something to hide. And we have nothing to hide. If we dropped the ball we'll admit it and apologise to the customer.

I was impressed with his cool demeanour and stoicism in the face of jagged criticism. Could I be as magnanimous if being criticised? Could you? It seems the ability to do so is a cornerstone of entrepreneurs' success.

As Booktopia's Tony Nash sagely puts it:

> I think it's very important not to identify with your business. You are not your business. If the business is criticised, you have to be able to separate yourself from your business.

Mark Middo, author of the book *5 Minute Business*, believes that 'if you're not being criticised, you're not trying hard enough or making enough mistakes'.

As the head of a publicly-listed company – Freelancer – Matt Barrie is well versed in dealing with cage-rattlers, but is ever the realist when asked how he deals with criticism: 'It depends who it comes from'.

In line with that, one of the best pieces of advice I ever heard from Harry M. Miller was, 'Choose who you listen to'.

Regrets: they've had a few, but then again, too few to mention

Unsurprisingly, being forward-looking people, very few of the entrepreneurs were expansive on this topic. 'Why would I regret learning something that has made my business better?' they'd say.

But surely there must be *something* they would have done differently?

When pressed, they answered, if not a little reluctantly, as follows.

Andre Eikmeier: I would have reached out to some mentors at the start – people who I really admire in the business.

Simon Griffiths: We'd have done things much more quickly: try to get to the end result as quickly as possible so that we could find out if we were doing something right or wrong. We could have then made the changes that we needed to get to the end result faster.

Stephanie Alexander: Based on sales and the amount of extra money it required to develop for both platforms, if I had my time over again, I wouldn't be on the Android app platform.

Jodie Fox: I'd recommend you do everything before you are ready. You just need to execute everything so fast and you need to be sharing it with your community so that they can help you develop a better product. I would have been much more data-oriented earlier on as well. It took me a little while to understand that and really bring that into my method of working.

Follow the leader

Like finding out who the Pope, Kim Kardashian or Kim Jong-Un follow on Twitter, I was curious to find out who the entrepreneurs looked up to, admired, respected.

Matt Barrie: Elon Musk. He was one of the early players in PayPal. He started the Tesla Electric Car Company and Space X, with the goal being to get to Mars. And now he's talking about a new form of transportation called the Hyperloop, which he thinks can get us from New York to San Francisco in half an hour or so. It's pretty amazing that one man has the drive and the inner fire to want to change humankind.

Stephanie Alexander: Jamie Oliver, because he can have his fingers in so many pies at once. And for having the cash flow to be able to engage the right people to make his projects flourish. Jamie employs well over 100 people, so it means that he can do all these other things and that money enables him to do more social entrepreneurship.

Andre Eikmeier: Seth Godin. He is philosophical, and he has got a real belief to make the world a better place, in a marketing sense. I admire Steve Jobs because he didn't compromise on the perfection of a product and his vision, which is really inspirational. He ignored short-term commercial pressures and went, 'No, I want this to be perfect'. I also admire the shoe company Zappos. They offer perfect customer service.

Simon Griffiths: A company in Kenya called Synergy. They try to figure out how to monetise sanitation, and how to sell toilet services to people that don't have them. They're incredibly inspiring because they essentially are looking at how to create a sustainable business model that solves a business problem that may someday be profitable, but may not.

Darren Rowse: Chris Guillebeau. He has a blog called 'The Art of Non-Conformity' and runs the conference 'World Domination Summit'. He has kept his values; he has the right community. He's got diversity in what he does, and he has multiple topics. He keeps a lid on things and he gives a lot back to his communities.

Recharge the batteries

So what do the entrepreneurs do for relaxation, to switch off, to recover from the long-haul flights, the endless meetings and the intense concentration that running a company requires?

> For fun, I crunch numbers.
> **Simon Griffiths**

Simon Griffiths' choice of relaxation is surprising.

> For fun, I crunch numbers. I run spreadsheets at 11:00 at night. I love getting into the accounting software and making everything neat so that I can see what our margin is. And that for me is what my passion is.

(Personally, I'd rather stick a needle in my eye than read spreadsheets at any time of the day but, as they say at personal development courses, 'We all have different preferences', which of course is just an acceptable way of saying 'You're nuts, mate!')

Tony Nash chooses to go for a jog, with no music, using the time to reflect on issues both personal and business. 'I find it quite peaceful. It's my form of meditation, I guess.'

Brian Shanahan, a busy father of three, believes you have to get out of the business to focus on the business.

> I like to spend a day of every fortnight out of the office. I usually go to the local library, put the headphones on and just do some of that 'quiet' thinking that needs to be done about where we have been, where we are today and where we want to go tomorrow.

Stephanie Alexander likes the simple pleasures: reading a good book, seeing a movie or having dinner with friends.

Bernadette: Do you ever get sick of cooking?

Stephanie: No, never.

I had to ask.

* * *

It's quite clear that successful entrepreneurs do things differently from others. They're able to reframe failure as feedback, are adept at taking action quickly and are comfortable with uncertainty.

They do what others aren't prepared to do and don't waste time poisoning their mind with 'poor me, look how hard I'm working' narratives that undermine their work and induce rationalisations of why success can't be theirs.

They're crystal clear about what their business does, what it stands for, what behaviour and attitudes they will tolerate and what they won't.

They can sum up their unique selling point in a heartbeat and can roll it out without it sounding rehearsed, insincere or disingenuous. They are way ahead of most people when it comes to which technology is around the corner and how that will affect their business. Like everyone, they dislike criticism but take it as feedback and are very cautious as to who they take it from.

They excel at time management and rarely look back with regret.

They take time to hire, but are quick to fire if the decision is flawed, and they take hiring very, very seriously. Hiring the best people is their number-one priority, and finding them their biggest headache.

What's next?

For those of you who are keen to get an online business up and running but just can't seem to get started, or if you have plenty of ideas but just can't decide which one to follow, the next chapter will make getting your business off the ground a whole lot easier.

CHAPTER THREE
PLANNING

> Don't let good be the enemy of great.
>
> *Russian saying*

Want an online business but can't get started?

We've all heard it. Maybe you've even said it. It's the cry of the 'I woulda-coulda-shoulda' brigade:

- 'I had that idea ages ago.'

- 'That was my idea!'

- 'I could've done that.'

Which begets the question, 'Why didn't you?'

We're all given the same amount of time in every day, yet some of us just seem to have a knack for squeezing more from it than others; for achieving our goals in spite of the fact we have [insert preferred excuse here: multiple children, no money to invest, no contacts in the business, no experience, no time, no family support, no education] ...

Planning is the key to success and by putting in some of these basic steps you'll find your business unfolding faster than you ever thought possible. But first, let's look at some of the reasons why most people fail to even get started.

What's stopping you from getting started?

There are dozens of reasons why people fail to succeed in business, but taking too long to start is one of them. Here are the top four ways we sabotage our businesses before we've even started.

> People get hung up on stupid things like business cards.
>
> **Kate Morris**

1. We focus on the wrong things

I was curious as to what holds entrepreneurs back from fulfilling their potential, or from taking the idea from a thought to reality. I asked Kate Morris, founder of the online beauty store Adore Beauty, what mistakes she sees would-be entrepreneurs make that stop them from getting started.

Kate: People get hung up on stupid things like business cards. I have conversations with people looking at starting a business and their biggest question is how their business card is going to be designed! Forget about your business cards. It doesn't matter. Just print them out yourself on your home computer.

Bernadette: So what should they be doing instead of tinkering with their cards?

Kate: All of your energy should be spent on looking at the fundamentals of your business and working out what you can be best in the world at; why customers are going to want to come to your business; how you will be different; how you will be better; and then how you are going to reach those customers. Forget about your logo and your business card. It's all secondary to what you should be focusing on.

2. We wait for perfection

Mark Middo, author of *5 Minute Business*, believes many people waste valuable time pursuing perfection, a trap for many would-be entrepreneurs.

> One multimillionaire entrepreneur I know says 'build a tractor first, then turn it into a Ferrari' and I think that's the best way to go. You've got to be out there first, getting some runs on the board and testing it, rather than trying to get the thing perfect before you even launch it. If you're happy with your first product then you've spent too long on it! Just keep making it better and better and the success will flow from that.

3. We get hung up on the technical side

James Tuckerman, founder of the leading entrepreneurial online magazine *Anthill Online* (www.anthillonline.com) says:

> When people are attempting to do something online and they can't work out the technical side, they become stressed out and paralysed. To overcome that, you need to use outsourcing sites to outsource it to people who can do the technical side for you. It would take two minutes for them to do it and save you a lot of heartache and stress, and it would cost you next to nothing compared to the time you'd take to figure it out yourself.

4. We want dozens of customers before we get one

Some of the most frequently asked questions I get from start-up business owners is, 'How can I find customers? How can I let people know my business exists?'

The frustration is palpable, especially for those with no marketing budget, no customers and no track record.

One of the key issues at the heart of this is the belief held by a lot of online business owners that 'if I just write one fantastic blog, I'll hit the jackpot and my database will explode…if I just get on one TV talk show, I'll be inundated with sales…if I just create one amazing video that goes viral, I'll get 10 000 Facebook fans overnight'.

'It just doesn't work that way,' says Mark Middo. 'There's only one real way to build a business, and that's one customer at a time.'

It reminds me of those money booths you see in game shows, where the contestant tries to catch as many of the notes as they can, hoping to grab big handfuls of them, and getting none when they would have been better off standing still, focusing and grabbing one note at a time. A bird in the hand, and all that.

Sometimes, people are so busy trying to dominate the market with media releases, events and multiple products, they forget that the essence of business is finding, and then serving, one customer. And then another. And then another. And, of course, one customer does lead to another.

Brian Shanahan, co-founder of the online homewares shopping club Temple & Webster, remembers clearly his very first customer.

> In the first few days after launch, we would watch every order that came through. The first one would be from say, Joe Smith, and I'd ask, 'Does anybody know Joe Smith?' and one of us around the table would put their hand up. 'What about Jane Brown? Does anybody know Jane Brown?' 'Yes I know Jane,' someone would say. So for the first day or so, it was just purchases from our very supportive friends. But I do remember that first transaction coming through from a 'Julie' from Main Beach in Queensland. 'Does anybody know Julie? ... No? ... Hurrah! A real customer! This is going to work!' And then more and more orders started to come in from people around Australia that we didn't know. It was high-fives all round. It was a great day.

So, focus on getting one customer and the rest will follow.

A helpful hint on how to get your online business started

Ready. Fire. Aim.

For most successful entrepreneurs, this is the mantra by which they live. 'Why waste time aiming,' they ask, 'when I can fire and get instant feedback? The feedback tells me what I have to do next'.

It's quite a devilishly simple concept but tough to deploy. Only those with absolute faith in themselves can pull it off because it takes guts to get things wrong, and to start again. But 'starting again' is not in their vernacular. They call starting again 'iterating' and it's a vital cog in the wheel of a start-up's success.

For the entrepreneurs I interviewed, the key to success begins with beginning, even if the idea is unclear, unformed or untested. The momentum that starting brings often provides valuable data that lights the way and indicates which direction should be taken next, like lanterns in the forest.

'Why is there so much power in just starting?' I asked Mark Middo, an expert at getting things moving fast.

> Because once something is up and people can look at it — a website, a video, a report, a white paper — you're getting *feedback*, you're getting traction and if it's out there for all to see, you can iterate your idea much faster. If people can't *see* it, they can't comment on it, good or bad, so the chances of you getting sales, investors or PR is severely diminished.

Simon Griffiths, founder of the online social enterprise Who Gives a Crap, says his motto is to act fast.

> Make mistakes, learn fast, adapt even faster and eventually you will end up with something that's successful or a complete failure, but you won't have spent all your time and all your money working on it.

How to research your idea to assess the demand

One of the major reasons people don't get started is because they either have one idea that they're completely obsessed with and can't bear to part with, or they have multiple ideas, all equally good, and can't decide which one to run with.

The key problem both face is that they generally don't have the tools or techniques to assess whether the idea has any merit, to identify whether it has a market or to evaluate the likelihood of success. Here's nine simple ways you can check to see if your idea is worth pursuing.

1. Check the search volumes

I asked Mark Middo for his strategies on how to assess whether a business idea is worth investing money and time in.

> A warning sign that your topic is *not* in hot demand would be if you checked it out on Google Keyword Planner and discovered there isn't much traffic going to that particular keyword.
>
> For example, let's say you had an idea for a natural therapy product—say, a specific acne cure—and you looked up how much that acne cure is getting searched on Google. If it isn't getting searched much, you'd know straight away there isn't much of a market for it.

2. Check the competition

It's worth checking out the competitors too, says Mark.

> You can use a site called www.similarweb.com. This allows you to check the traffic numbers of particular websites that are in competition to you. You could pop any website in and look up the competitors that appear as number one for that particular industry and see how much traffic they are getting. If it shows no data and there is not much traffic coming through, then you can pretty much estimate that there is not going to be a huge demand for that product.
>
> You can also check the Fan Page numbers on the Facebook pages of the competitors in your niche area. You can set up a Facebook ad and then go to the Advertising section on Facebook, use the Targeting or Profiling filters, and see how many people are in the market for that product. You can pop in keywords there as well and they will tell you how many you'll reach on Facebook.

3. Check out what's hot or not

James Tuckerman, founder of the successful entrepreneur membership site Anthill Online has a good tip for finding out what's hot.

> To find out what topics are 'hot', you can type any topic into www .buzzsumo.com and it will show you the most shared content using that keyword. This is really useful. You can also type in your own URL or a competitor's and find out what is being shared on their site.

After a while you will begin to see that certain types of content are getting shared a lot and you will pick your niche. You begin to see the trends.

4. Check out the trends

Darren Rowse, founder of ProBlogger and worldwide authority on all things bloggy, recommends Google Trends.

You can type in any keyword and it will show you whether the search volumes are increasing or decreasing for that particular word, which is really helpful. You can also compare words to see if a word is more powerful than another.

For example, if you look up Digital Photography versus Film Photography you can see if one is declining or if one is increasing and you can see what search demand is for those terms. This will help you when naming your products, as you want to use popular search terms.

Or do a search on Amazon and see how many books are being published on that topic. That will tell you whether those books are doing well and if there is a demand for that topic.

5. Check out what people are talking about

Darren recommends eavesdropping too.

When I started, I didn't do much research but went on a hunch or noticed a rising demand. It's important to listen to conversations with your friends or just read the news. I also recommend simple things like just going to a local newsagent and noticing what magazines have been published.

6. Check out what your friends think

Jodie Fox, founder of Shoes of Prey, keeps it simple too. She tested her business idea by asking her target market what they thought. They were easy to reach: they were her girlfriends.

An excellent way to test your idea or validate your market is to write a survey, share it with your friends and get them to pass it on to as many people as possible. It may sound really simple but it's the fastest, easiest way to get feedback on your idea without spending a lot of money.

We did that with Shoes of Prey before we launched and it gave us some great insights into what the market wanted that we wouldn't have perhaps thought of.

I asked Jodie what the minimum sample size should be.

You'll need to send it to at least 100 people in the target market to make it worthwhile. I then recommend you look at the size of the market, look at how that market is behaving and gather statistics so that you can assess if the market, and the opportunity, is big enough.

Darren Rowse has some simple but clever strategies.

You need to find out where your customers are online, so we survey our readers and ask, 'What social media are you using?' That informs us where they hang out as well. We just want to be as useful as possible so we only share links to useful stuff that we know people will like and share, and that then helps us to go further and be better on Facebook.

Tip
Use www.surveymonkey.com to run free surveys on your market.

For example, if you sign up for our newsletter, we'll send you an email saying, 'You have been registered for a while now and we would love to learn a little bit more about you'. This helps us get a bit of demographic information and then we also ask them about topics that they want us to write about on the blog and also questions about what sort of things they would pay for. We test out our theories but we also watch how blog posts go down with our audiences as well.

7. Check engagement levels on your blogs

Darren believes tracking levels of engagement with your blogs can lead to valuable insights.

One time, we had a series of blog posts on posing for portraits and they just went wild. When that went well, we were pretty sure we wanted to do an eBook on that particular topic. That is the advantage of having a blog — you can be testing your ideas by writing a short blog post and it will give you a feel as to whether the audience wants more on that. And from time to time, we put a 'call out' on social media for questions or problems that people are facing and try and gauge their interest on those topics that way.

8. Check out what else is already selling

Darren Rowse has a sample size of five million readers to work with, so when he does a survey, you can be pretty sure the answers are representative of what the market thinks. But even if you only have a small database, it's still worth trying. Any insight is a good insight, he says.

A good way to test whether a product might work with the audience is to recommend someone else's product first. That's what I did. I was recommending eBooks before I made eBooks so I knew right away what my audience bought and I knew what topics they were buying. So that's a nice and easy way to test out what is going to work.

9. Check out what's selling on eBay and for how much

Shaun O'Brien suggests using eBay as a research tool.

Whether you want to sell on eBay or not it's a good benchmark of what your price point needs to be. As a standalone website eBay is going to be your biggest competitor no matter what, particularly in Australia, so it's worth knowing who is selling what and for how much. Amazon is a good cross-check as well.

Test your idea: share and talk

If you were one of those kids who got told off for talking in class all the time — like I was — I've got good news for you. Having the gift of the gab may just be your biggest asset. Don't hesitate to 'talk up' your ideas to the world and don't make the rookie mistake of thinking everyone's going to steal them. They won't.

Here's a scenario that I come across all the time from people seeking advice on how to get their online business started:

I once MC'd an event for online entrepreneurs and after the event a well-dressed, 30-something woman approached me, seeking my advice.

'I have an idea that I would like to turn into a business, but I don't know where to start,' she said, softly, afraid of being overheard.

'Okay, what are you selling?'

Her eyes darted around the room, 'I don't want to say too much at this stage as it's early days ... but it's to do with fashion.'

'Okaaaay, what sort of fashion?' I asked, drilling down to get some idea of how I could help her.

'Handbags,' she whispered.

'Right, and can you tell me a bit more?'

She paused. 'I can't say too much, but what I really want to know is how can I protect my idea. It's quite unique.'

'What sort of idea are you wanting to protect?'

'I can't tell you,' she said.

You'd be amazed at how often this scenario unfolds. Here's what I feel like saying (but don't):

Save your breath sister. Here's the thing: if I'm going to run off with an idea, raise $5 million in capital to fund it, put my life on hold for three years while I bring it to life, spend the next two years travelling the world to spruik it, quite possibly bankrupting me and my family in the process just so I can bring an idea to life, it's going to be *my* idea!

Jordan Green, an angel investor and founder of Melbourne Angels (www.melbourneangels.net) is very clear about the benefits of talking about your ideas.

> How can you get people on board to your idea if you don't tell them about it? Sure, you can get people to sign NDAs but really, ideas are nothing, ideas have no value at all. It's all in the execution. And when people invest in your business, they're not just investing in the idea, they're investing in *you*, and your team, if you have one. You need to be someone they want to be in business with. You need to represent solidity and be someone they feel they can work with.

Jodie Fox of Shoes of Prey concurs.

> The first thing is to just talk to as many people about your idea and get as much feedback as you can about your idea before you begin. Secondly, look at the businesses that are doing well, even if they're not your competitors. Thirdly, read the blogs written by other entrepreneurs. They share their stories very openly and you can learn a lot from that.

'But who can I share my idea with?' I hear you say. 'No-one wants to hear my story again. Where can I find people willing to listen?'

Here's four great ways to test your idea and get instant feedback to see if it has traction.

1. Attend hackathons

One of the best ways to test your idea is to be among like-minded people.

Toby Tremayne, a programmer and tech entrepreneur, says:

> No matter what your experience, hackathons are a great way to get a quick feel for what it takes to build a product or a platform, and an opportunity to discover whether that kind of work appeals to you. Even if you're not a tech, you'll learn a lot about building a modern business and get to meet the kind of people you'll need to make a start-up successful.

Jodie Fox agrees. 'These workshops compress your timeline and highlight the friction points.'

And a friction point would be...

> Anything that stops you from getting started. They could be as simple as 'I don't know where to find a good IP (intellectual property) lawyer' or 'I don't know how to set up a company structure' or it could be as complex as 'sales have unexpectedly dropped off this quarter and I don't know why'. Then you have to set about solving the problem and getting to the root issue of what caused it.

Harry M. Miller used to say, 'If you've got an idea or a product and you need help, stand on top of a mountain and shout about it as loud as you can!' It wasn't the most sophisticated strategy, but as an old-style theatrical impresario who sold millions of tickets to his stage-musical blockbusters, he knew what he was talking about. Get out there and tell the world!

Harry used to walk into the office and, apropos of nothing, just yell out 'Does anyone know someone who can install a lift?' Ah, no Harry, not off the top of my head.

'What about a private plane? I need one tomorrow. Find me one.' He didn't assume anything and sincerely believed that by just saying it, as often and as loud as he could, that someone, somewhere, might have the answer. And it got results. We'd all furrow our brows, desperately hoping we knew someone who could install a lift! Now, of course, we use social media to get recommendations, but just letting people in your immediate vicinity know what you need can be just as powerful. People love to feel they're being helpful. When in doubt, just shout it out to whoever will listen.

2. Run it as a short course

Running a short course at a local TAFE or community college on your topic (if relevant) is one of the cheapest, fastest ways to test your idea, get real-time feedback and see who's in your target market.

Paula is a hooker. Well, not anymore, but she was, and a good one by all accounts—a high-class one. 'What an oxymoron,' she'd say ruefully.

Paula's had a tough life and after leaving 'the industry' she struggled to get proper paid work that wasn't as, shall we say, strenuous. But one thing she learned as a working girl was that there are lots of young men out there desperate for a shag with a snowball's chance in hell of getting one, for all sorts of reasons, which we won't go into here.

So after brainstorming a few ideas of what she could do to turn her life around and use her knowledge of men to good effect, she came up with the idea that there's a need to teach young men how to 'be' with a woman. Not just 'be' in the biblical sense, but 'be' as in how to be a gentleman, how to be chivalrous when dining at a restaurant, how to be civil when a girl rejects him, how to be a good listener and partner, and all sorts of other things.

She put together the course curriculum, pitched it to a local community college and lo and behold, they put it on, and now the course, and her business, is going gangbusters. She's turned her life around, earns decent dough and helps lots of young men form satisfying, loving and mutually rewarding interpersonal relationships. And with their newfound confidence, they are possibly getting a shag too. A happy ending all round.

So what can we learn from Paula's 'finishing school for young men' and what does that have to do with online entrepreneurship?

Lots. You see, Paula could have built a website, written loads of brochures, bought a database list and advertised on websites to build her business. But instead, all she did was invest three minutes on the phone to pitch the idea to the course coordinator and she was off and running. They advertised it for her in the course brochure, provided the venue, took the bookings, managed the customer service and more. All she had to do was turn up and deliver the course.

If people didn't enrol, all she lost was a few hours in time putting the curriculum together.

If people *did* enrol – which they did – then she had a winner on her hands and she could use the experience to iterate the idea and make the next version better, and, best of all, she got paid to do it too.

3. Commit publicly to a deadline

When I sold my first home-study copywriting pack, the manual (the cornerstone of the pack) was by no means finished. 'But how can that be?' I hear you say. 'You said you sold it two days after launching.' And I did. But the manual was not finished. As Paul Greenberg says, quoting from Shakespeare's *Hamlet*, 'to thine own self be true'. Well, I knew my true weakness was completion and perfectionism (a devilish twosome) so instead of holding onto it and trying to make it perfect, I sold it and told my new students that it was Part One, and that Part Two, the last 10 chapters, would come 'very soon'.

This strategy of promoting a product before it's finished has multiple benefits.

- It helps to see what the demand for it is – if there's no-one wanting it, what's the point of creating it?

- For me, it enabled me to complete Part Two with a bit of breathing space so that I could finish it to a standard with which I would be happy.

- It committed me to completing the task.

I knew that to *not* complete Part Two would mean I would:

- disappoint the students who had bought it

- have to give them their money back

- find another way to replace the income I'd foregone by being a stay-at-home mum.

Three big reasons to keep going. And it worked.

PS: Did the students mind getting the course in two parts? No, not a bit. I told them what I was doing and they already had 350 pages to go on with. The motto? Communicate, be honest and, most times, people will be more than accommodating.

4. Create a prototype and send it to your target market
Simon Griffiths followed a similar approach.

> When it comes to testing anything, it's all about prototyping. We needed to make sure that people would buy toilet paper online, so we set up a Shopify store for 40 bucks. We went to the supermarket, bought a bunch of toilet paper, found some boxes, packaged toilet paper up in boxes and then started mailing it to people, which cost us a stupid amount of money, but it allowed us to test whether people would actually respond to the opportunity to buy toilet paper online.

> The nature of our business is that we're not a Silicon Valley start-up that has millions of dollars behind us. So everything we do is bootstrapped. We have to do everything ourselves, for the first time at least, to figure out if it's going to work.

Get it up and running!
Having the courage to put your product in the marketplace is the only real way to find out if people want it or not. Here are some helpful tips and suggestions on how you can take constructive action to find a product and get it into the market place.

Find a product or service to sell
In order to sell a product or service, you have to first find one, and that involves making a decision. The true meaning of 'decide' is to 'cut off' so all that really matters at this point is that you commit fully to whatever you decide to sell, and cut off all other options. You then put it out in the marketplace and see what happens. Here's five strategies to get you started.

1. Create a Minimum Viable Product (MVP)

Andre Eikmeier, co-founder of the online wine retailer Vinomofo says:

> You've got to get honest feedback from the market. It's about creating a Minimum Viable Product so that you've got something to sell that you can afford to make, and the more refined the product is, the more use it's going to be to someone—rather than offering a broad product that's really not well developed and thought out.

But what is exactly is a Minimum Viable Product? According to Andre, it means:

> What's the soonest I can get this product out there and it still be useful to people? It's about not being hung up on it being perfect before you start selling it. So you might have a master plan, but you can't activate it at that early stage.

> With Vinomofo we know what the perfect site is but that's three years away. We are not going to get there tomorrow, but we can't sit there waiting for this perfect product to arrive. Of course, we are well aware that the first impression may not be good and people may not respond, but you've got to let go of that and get started. For us, it was about 'let's just get one wine onto the website per day, get it out there in email and see how it goes'. It's about speed to market.

2. Jump on a plane

If you want to source product from overseas, just get on a plane and go find it. You can use Alibaba.com or any of its subsidiaries to source a product, but no amount of emailing or Skyping will substitute for being on the ground, meeting the people and checking the quality.

Brad Smith, founder of the motorbike and accessories retailer braaap (Motorcycles) knew he wanted to import motorbikes, so he got on a plane to China, visited dozens of factories in person, talked to each owner—even though he couldn't speak the language—and after the umpteenth factory visit, he knew enough Mandarin to make himself understood and choose the right factory. He had to eyeball the owner to work out if the partnership was going to work. He found the people he needed and he's been importing products happily ever since.

3. Be hands-on

Dean Ramler, co-founder of the online designer furniture store Milan Direct, discovered that being hands-on pays off.

> We opened the first container of furniture on the docks and before I signed off on the container I checked everything to make sure that what I ordered was what I got and discovered that the furniture was not what we ordered. If I had not been hands-on and picked this up, I would have signed off on the inventory and it could well have shut us down before we even got started.

4. Make people pay for it

Mark Middo says:

> The quickest way to test an idea is to get it out to the market to see if people want it. You can research it 'til the cows come home, but until you have a product or a service that people are willing to pay you money for, you don't have a business.

Andre Eikmeier recommends treating the sales process like a conversation.

> Say, 'I've created this thing, I'd love to get your feedback on it' and treat it as the beta audience phase. People appreciate being invited to come along on this journey. In fact, it's better to put it out there for sale rather than ask for their opinion, because people put on a different hat when they are being asked for feedback and advice. It's better to just get it out and say, 'Here is the product' and see if people pay for it or not.

5. Create an information product (like an eBook)

A great way to get started before you invest money and time into the business is to create an eBook to check on the demand and, as a side benefit, help build your database.

Once you've got your eBook ready, you can set up a pay-per-click campaign for $10 a day or so, and use that medium to drive traffic to your landing page. This helps you build a list of interested prospects. It also enables you to test the various eBook headlines to see which works best and to test the demand for the topic.

For those of you selling information products, Mark Middo has some good ideas on how to build one quickly.

Q & A with Mark Middo on how to create an information product quickly

If you'd like to create and sell your own information, you can't go past the king of content creation, Mark Middo. He's created a host of information products so I was keen to find out how he did it.

Bernadette: What tips would you give to people wanting to sell informational products online?

Mark: The key to selling informational products is to find a good niche. You need to find something that has lots of pain behind it that people are prepared to spend money on to fix.

Bernadette: People have lots of good ideas on what they can sell, but what's the best way to research a niche? Is there a tool we can use?

Mark: A good way to find a niche that is untapped is to use HubPages (www.hubpages.com) and see what the most popular articles are in those particular niches. HubPages is a user-generated content, revenue-sharing website. It hosts internet content created by its members on a vast array of different topics.

Bernadette: How does it work?

Mark: For example, if you had a health eBook you wanted to sell, you'd click on HubPages, look up the 'health' section and see what articles are really popular.

You might find an article that's popular about some new Japanese technique that helps people lose weight and start researching it further via Facebook fan pages to see if it's trending anywhere else. If it's looking like it has a following, you'd dig deeper to find out what other competitive products are available, and then develop a product on the topic.

Bernadette: Are there any untapped niches still left?

Mark: There are heaps! There are a lot of niches where people started websites five to ten years ago and their websites look old and tired but are ranking highly on Google because they've been around so long. So you can enter into these niches with your brand new website—which you made on WordPress (www.wordpress.org) for just $50 and which looks better than the others, and people will start buying your products instead of theirs. Check out Flippa (www.flippa .com.au) to see what websites are available for sale. They're like the eBay of websites where you can buy and sell used and new websites.

Bernadette: Can you share some of those 'hot niches' with us?

Mark: I think there's a lot of room for exploration in the alternative therapies area, like yoga for men. I think that's a hot niche for someone to really tap into because once upon a time, yoga was seen as a very female activity, but a lot of guys want to do it but feel that it's a bit too girly. That's a massive opportunity for someone who wants to go out and write an eBook on how to make yoga more sporty and masculine and attractive to men.

Bernadette: How can an eBook help people make money?

Mark: First up, you need a free product to give away to get people onto your list so that you can then sell them the next-level product. That's what we call a 'product for prospect' such as an eBook or report. You want to make this a good product that you can give away or sell very, very cheaply. Once you have them in your sales funnel and they've bought the cheaper product, you can upsell high-end items and that's where you can really start to make money on your informational products.

How to get your online business up and running without leaving full-time work

Earlier, we discussed whether people should leave their day job and just jump into their new business, or hedge their bets and transition from full-time work to part-time work.

I always recommend my copywriting students keep working at whatever they're doing and try to build up their business on the side. I encourage them to think about how they can use their existing workplace as an 'incubator' of sorts, a 'test lab' in which to try out their business idea or build their skillset so when they do leave, they've got a strong base from which to work.

To get the best results from creating an incubator for your new business at your old business, work out what skillsets you're missing and what you need to learn.

Here are three ways I've seen my students develop their new business while learning a new skill and enjoying the security of a pay cheque.

1. Develop website skills

Every entrepreneur would benefit from learning how to build a website using WordPress.

So why not learn how to build your own website on the company penny by offering to build or redesign your boss's website? Can they send you to a WordPress training course? Will they pay for you to do an SEO (search engine optimisation) course to help their site get to the top of Google? So long as you're helping them first, then it's just a bonus that you're winning too.

2. Develop content creation skills

Every company has a website so why not ask if you can help create content for it? If not, what about creating content for the staff newsletter, drafting the Christmas party flyer, or writing up some case studies?

They get a much-needed job done without having to pay any extra and you get to add to your portfolio, gain valuable experience and confidence and win a few brownie points in the process.

If you're not working for a company, offer to help out at a local kindergarten, football club or service organisation like Rotary. You could help them write their fundraising flyers, newsletter or website. They'd greet you with open arms.

3. Develop coding skills

If you want to upskill in coding or programming, offer to build and develop an app for the company you work for in exchange for them sending you to an app training course. Win–win. You get a professional development opportunity that will enhance your business idea. The company gets a new app developed by a staff member who already knows the business inside out.

PS: There are also some great incubator programs run through private enterprise and the universities, and these can be great testing grounds for start-ups. Many offer mentoring and practical support like offices, administrative assistance and funding to get you through those early days.

Get good at completion

One of the key lessons I've learned from interviewing successful entrepreneurs is that they excel at *completion*; that is, getting things done. They might not do everything themselves. What matters is that things get completed.

Tip

Don't wait for perfection to get started.

I asked Andre Eikmeier from Vinomofo why some people can get the ball rolling while others procrastinate.

> There is a real inclination when you are starting something that you've put your heart and soul into that you become too afraid to sell it! It's a common fear to just stay in the product development phase and try to perfect it because it's too painful to go out there and sell it if you're not proud of it.

You're thinking, 'I've got to get this perfect!' and that's not the case at all. Far from it. You've got to get it out of your head and get it out there and say, 'Hey! I have created this thing and I want feedback on this straight away' and the only honest feedback you can get is if people are willing to pay for it. You've got to get to that stage fast and early and before your product is ready. You're going to make mistakes. Accept that. Just try to make them faster so that you can get to where you're going sooner.

We've touched on procrastination already, but it's such an important topic, we'll cover it in more detail here.

Top 3 reasons why entrepreneurs procrastinate

Having coached hundreds of students in the art of writing, surely one of the most procrastinated-over activities on the planet (hasn't everybody got a half-finished novel in their bottom drawer?), I've got a few theories on why we don't finish things—not just writing projects, but anything, especially when they're important to us.

In fact, I would go so far as to say that sometimes it's the *really* important things we procrastinate over the most, simply because we care so much about them. What do you procrastinate over that you know is costing you money?

It could be:

- finishing the guest blog that will showcase your work to thousands of readers—if you could just get around to finishing the last paragraph

- finding that last pay slip the bank needs to see before they approve your business loan—if you could just get around to asking HR to print it off for you

- sending the client that quote they asked for, which, if approved, would pay your PA's salary for a year—if you could just get around to writing up the quote.

My take on the top three reasons why people don't complete tasks is because they:

- fear success

- fear failure

- have unclear objectives.

And this is the negative self-talk that goes along with these:

- *Fear of success*: 'I don't want to finish it because if I do and it goes out to the world, it might actually work and then I'll have to deal with the success it brings.'

- *Fear of failure*: 'I don't want to finish it because if I do and it goes out to the world, it might not work and then I'll have to deal with the feeling of rejection it brings.'

- *Unclear objectives*: 'I don't want to finish it because the project is so big I don't even know where to start.'

The reason I know these to be true is because I've suffered from all three. I can even *feel* the affliction coming on sometimes, particularly when it's an important job that I really value. When it comes to self-sabotage, I'm up there with the best, and if you've got any unfinished tasks or unaccomplished dreams, then you probably are too.

Avoid the pursuit of perfection

I have three humble but effective strategies that help me overcome my issues with incompleteness-ness. They sound ridiculously simple, but they really work for me and have worked for lots of my students too.

1. Complete, complete, complete!

In my office, I have a sticky note stuck to the front of my computer, and on it I've written three words: 'Complete, complete, complete'. Yeah, I know it sounds crazy, but I have to tell you that viewing those three words really helps me deal with obstacles. When I see it, it reminds me of my tendency to get distracted, and forces me to push through and complete what I'm doing.

2. Reward yourself

When my energy is flagging, but I know I have to finish a piece of work, I sometimes book myself a reward as an incentive to finish it. It might be a facial, a massage or a Gold Class movie. Knowing there is a reward at the end of 60 minutes, six hours or six days helps me overcome the lethargy that often sets in when I'm trying to finish something difficult or tedious.

When I have a big project to finish, I book a mini-holiday because nothing focuses my mind like a Jetstar departure time.

3. The five-minute rule: have courage

I got this technique from Todd Samson of the ABC program *The Gruen Transfer.* He believes that success is not about talent, but about overcoming fear—having courage. He tells the story of how people who really make things happen are those who have the courage to push through the 'five-minute fear barrier'. In other words, if you can keep going for just five minutes longer than the next person, no matter what the task is—writing, running, researching, meditating—then you'll push through to another level and reach a new plateau of accomplishment, which unleashes a new burst of energy. Often success is just the difference of five more minutes.

Tip

If you have a big project to finish, book a mini-holiday because nothing focuses the mind like a Jetstar departure time.

Keep up

If you're going to be an online entrepreneur, you're going to have to get familiar with the entrepreneur lingo.

- 'We have some friction points' means 'We have a problem'.

- 'We needed to pivot' means 'We made a mistake and had to make some changes'.

- 'We went through a series of iterations' means 'We tried lots of different things and none of them worked'.

* * *

Planning might sound boring, but it's the single most important factor for setting yourself up for success

Testing your market, assessing demand, running surveys and sharing your ideas are all fabulous ways to see if your idea has traction.

Or consider running it as a short course or create a Minimum Viable Product to see if people will pay you for it.

One cheap and easy way to test your idea is to create an eBook on the topic and sell it as best you can.

And once you've got clarity on your idea, investigate your existing workplace to see if there's any opportunity for them to help you incubate the business until you're ready to leave the security of a regular pay cheque.

And finally, have courage to keep going, as just five minutes more can be the difference between success and failure.

What's next?

If you're out to make a profit from your online endeavour, then check out the next chapter to find out how the entrepreneurs did it. They reveal the different business models they use, the merits of each, how they use pricing to position their products, how to source investors, and much more.

CHAPTER FOUR
PROFIT

Happiness lies not in the mere possession of money;
it lies in the joy of achievement, in the thrill of creative effort.

Franklin D. Roosevelt

The online gold rush

This chapter is about how to make money from an online business. You'll discover how the entrepreneurs I've interviewed made their money, the business models they chose, why they chose them, the merits of those models, how to source investors, what to look for in an investor and much more.

Few would disagree that we are in the midst of a social and technological revolution. We are living in uncharted territory, some likening it to the days of the gold rush when riches were to be found simply by digging a hole in the right place at the right time. In many ways, we're experiencing an online gold rush of sorts right now. What else can you call it when Mark Zuckerberg, a university dropout, can create a multi-billion dollar company in just eight years? Look at the host of associated industries that have been spawned as a result of Zuckerberg's creation and you can see that indeed a rising tide lifts all boats.

Let's take the gold rush analogy a bit further.

It's a little-known fact that in any gold rush, it's not just the pan-handlers mining for gold who get rich. It's the merchants who sell the miners the pans, the pick axes, the tents and the shovels who get extremely rich too, and certainly with less effort. While the miners braved the wind and cold, sifting through silt and soil on the off-chance of striking gold, the merchants had already struck it, counted it and banked it and were snuggled up nice and warm in their beds, dreaming about how much money they would make when the next round of speculators hit town.

Why were these merchants able to profit so effortlessly, while the miners struggled? They profited because they *anticipated* what the miners needed – food, drink, tools, guns – long before the miners knew they needed it themselves. The merchants' 'depth of vision', their ability to see not what is, but what's possible, enabled them to position themselves favourably before the miners even arrived.

The miners speculated. The merchants anticipated. The difference? Preparation. Knowledge.

Can we as entrepreneurs not do the same? Can we prepare ourselves to be in the right place at the right time to take future advantage of the boom that's occurring right now? What knowledge can we access that will give us the edge to predict what the next wave of speculators will need?

To help you get a glimpse into what those likely trends might be, I asked my friend and colleague Morris Miselowski, a business and technology futurist, to identify what he considers to be some life-changing trends that will open up a world of opportunity to entrepreneurs with depth of vision.

Morris's top 10 trends to watch

Take a look at what the future holds and see if you can anticipate the products and services we may need when these trends hit.

Food

By 2025, 80 per cent of all restaurants will use a 3D food printer as part of their usual meal preparation. NASA is about to send a 3D printer into space that will be able to print food, including pizzas, for astronauts.

Manufacturing

'Baxter' is an industrial robot with strong, moveable arms and a flat-screen display for a head. 'He' can be set up almost anywhere and is capable of learning any repetitive task within 90 seconds. He can then repeat it over and over again. He costs just US$26000.

Education

By 2020, 'Learning Analytic' will be the backbone of most classrooms. It will digitally intervene between students and teachers and monitor in real time each student's ability to engage and understand the lesson. It will routinely change the learning tools and instructions, automatically selecting the ones most appropriate to the student's learning style and needs.

Lawyers/accountants/service industry

Statutory paperwork and routine regulatory forms will all be completed digitally by 2025, leaving service providers to earn their fees by selling their wisdom, intuition and feelings.

As the sea of data rises and possibilities exponentially grow, we will be crying out for wise people to make sense and purpose

(continued)

Morris's top 10 trends to watch (cont'd)

out of it all for us. We'll be searching for experts who can let us know—in advance of us even knowing we need to know it—what to do about it or with it. That's tomorrow's service industry's goldmine.

Homes

By 2025, builders will routinely use 3D printers to convert digital drawings and specifications into homes, offices and factories. We will use large, multistorey gantry-mounted printers (similar to those seen on our shipping docks that pick up and move the large containers) that go backwards and forwards, floor by floor, printing layer by layer.

Digital payments

By 2030, crypto currencies like bitcoin will account for 15 per cent of all global financial transactions as we move ever closer to a less-cash, no-plastic-credit-card, global-currency world.

Universities

By 2030, 50 per cent of our traditional universities will have disappeared and an entirely new educational market will evolve, offering global qualifications, nano degrees (degrees in one skill only) and micro colleges where within six months you'll be able to learn and qualify for a new profession.

Medical

By 2050, we will routinely live to 100 and our children to 150 years of age. Much of this will be brought about by our move away from a medical system that focuses on repairing our bodies to a system that instead works 24/7 to maintain our health and wellbeing. This will be done by receiving real-time data from myriad wearable and implanted devices we routinely carry that inform us and our chosen health-provider ecosystem about what's happening inside us and what we have to do to maintain optimum health.

Fashion

Not sure what to wear, what colour outfit you need or whether it's going to be warm or cool out? Don't worry, by 2025 your clothes will be able to change colour, texture and pattern on demand. And forget about taking a jumper with you if you're cold, because your clothes will signal the room to change temperature, or if you're out and about the sensor will adjust the heating or cooling of the clothes you're wearing.

Travel

No time for a real holiday? How about a virtual one instead? Jump into your nearest travel digital *holideck*, lie down in your fringed virtual ocean cabana with a real margarita in one hand and enjoy the virtual sun shining down on you (sunscreen not required). Feel the virtual wind coming off the water, smell the ocean all around, hear the waves lapping up on the shore in front of you and slowly feel the real world disappear as you spend a sun-filled, stress-free day at your secluded virtual beach.

What business model will you choose?

The question, 'What is your business model?' is just a fancy way of asking 'How will your business make money?'

We've already looked at how to research and test a business idea, so assuming you now have clarity on the industry, category or topic you're going to focus on, let's look at some of the ways you can make money from it.

Part and parcel of choosing your business model is deciding whether you'll sell online products or online services.

Tip

'What is your business model?' is just a fancy way of asking 'How will your business make money?'

What's easier to sell: a tangible product or an intangible service?

I get asked this a lot, and it's a good question.

The truth is they both have their advantages and disadvantages. You see, it's not really about the product or service at all. It's about *you*. Specifically, about how you evaluate and explain value to your prospect. For example, some people are more comfortable selling a product they can touch, feel and experience, whereas others are more comfortable selling services they can sell via the story, the words and the images.

The easy answer is that no-one can answer this question for you. You have to go out and try it yourself. When you finally find the answer that's right for you, it will not come down to whether or not you're selling physical goods, but whether or not your experiences and biases will help you to identify and communicate the value proposition effectively.

Do you want to *sell* designer fashion or do you want to *teach* people how be a fashion designer?

Whether you decide to sell products or services, I can guarantee at some point you'll suffer from the 'grass is greener' syndrome. Take Simon, for example.

Simon is a fashion designer who makes his own original garments and imports vintage clothing. He sells both via his online store and from his bricks-and-mortar store in an inner-city suburb.

He rises at 5 am to check what orders have arrived overnight and heads into the shop to open at 9 am.

'Sometimes I think it'd be easier to *teach* people how to be a fashion designer rather than *sell* designer fashion. If I sold an information product instead of a real product, I wouldn't have to worry about what Top Shop and Zara are doing, about having stock left over at the end of the season or about paying rent, wages and insurances. Nor would I have to get up every day and battle the traffic to come in to the shop! To cap it off, I've had two new fashion shops open up on the same street in the past three months. Sometimes I think selling an online service would be so much easier.'

Now compare Simon's scenario with Simonne's.

Simonne is a fashion designer who offers an online education and mentoring program to up-and-coming fashion designers. She sells her services via online channels.

'Sometimes I think it'd be easier to *sell* people designer fashion rather than *teach* them how to be a fashion designer.

'If I sold real clothing, something people could see and touch, I wouldn't have been up 'til 3 am this morning recording new videos for my coaching program. I also wouldn't have to constantly create new content for my blog or my podcast, nor would I have to write endless auto-responder emails to keep the conversion rates up. To cap it off, a famous American fashion designer from a reality TV show has just created a new online coaching program, so now I have to compete with yet another designer who has a higher profile than me.

Sometimes I think selling a real, tangible product that people can see, feel and experience would be so much easier.'

So before you make your decision, know that there will always be advantages and disadvantages, no matter what.

Online products vs online services: what's easier to sell?

Online products and online services both have merit and I'll outline here my perspective on the respective merits of both.

Table 4.1 shows the pros and cons of selling products online (that is, *tangible* items such as books, clothing, toys, shoes and computers).

Table 4.1: pros and cons of selling products online

Pros	Cons
Real, touchable, easy to display and promote	The cost of goods
Price is easily compared with others on the market; less 'smoke and mirrors' about value	Price is checkable so people can haggle you down
Price is generally not based on perceived value (unless it's in the high-end or luxury goods market)	The business is not scalable: whether you sell 10 or 10000, you still have to buy each and every product

Table 4.2 shows the pros and cons of selling online services such as software, education programs and web design (that is, intangible items).

Table 4.2: pros and cons of selling online services

Pros	Cons
Can be relatively easy and cost-effective to create	Price/value is hard to define and communicate
No cost of goods (except production and design)	Easily consumed and copied and may still need to be refunded
No delivery fees	Needs updating to keep content fresh and relevant
Scalable: it's as cost-effective to sell 10 as it is 10000	You need a big database to get traction
Price is not easily compared: more 'smoke and mirrors' about value	Perceived value is subject to 'smoke and mirrors'

As you can see, for every pro there is also a con; you need to decide what you feel most comfortable selling.

How to turn any product or service into an information product

If you're a service provider such as a coach, a counsellor or an accountant, you may be thinking, 'I'd like to learn how to convert my expert knowledge on this topic into an information product that I can sell online'.

Conversely, if you sell products such as clothing, computers or cars, you may also be thinking, 'I'd like to learn how to convert my expert knowledge on this topic into an information product that I can sell online'.

As you can see, irrespective of whether you sell a service or a product, you can still create an information product to sell online.

Here's how.

For those who sell services

Most service providers operate under the limiting time-for-money model ('I give you an hour of my time and you pay me an hourly rate'). As we all know, this limits your income to the number of hours in a day you can work, and even if you have staff, you're still limited by the number of hours they can work. So what can you do?

If you're in a service business where you don't physically sell a product such as clothing, pens or computers, you may want to consider turning your knowledge, wisdom and processes into online information products so that you can monetise your intellectual knowledge, offer a scalable product and move away from the time-for-money model that is the bane of every service professional's life.

> **Tip**
> Successful information sellers create 'processes' that position the owner of the process as the expert in that topic.

To do this successfully, you'll need to develop a systematised process that is uniquely yours. Think of all the famous processes developed over the years that take what is essentially an idea and convert it into a 'system'. For example:

- Stephen Covey's 'Seven Habits of Highly Effective People' training programs

- the Six Sigma Black Belt certification

- the MBTI personality profile tool

- Tony Robbins' 30-day transformation programs.

Successful information sellers create 'processes' that position the owner of the process as the expert in that business. Your 'process' becomes your unique intellectual property (IP), which now becomes your product.

For those who sell products

If you sell a tangible product but want to have an information product too, you just need to find a nugget of unique wisdom that you can turn into a process.

For example, if you've built a fashion business into a successful operation, there are bound to be other fashion operators who want to know your secrets. Why not create a process around your IP and build a product around that – maybe an eBook called *How I Built a Multimillion-dollar Fashion Empire from Nothing in Just Five Years.* You'll want to have a back-end product like a coaching or mentoring service to take advantage of the leverage the eBook creates. Or you may just want to use the eBook to attract more customers, investors or media attention.

Information products come in lots of different formats, such as:

- eBooks and reports

- membership sites

- hardcopy books

- DVDs and CDs

- email newsletters

- apps.

Examples of these formats include:

- *coaching programs:* 'How to Become a Millionaire Overnight: download your 12-month webinar series now'

- *beginner's guides:* 'The beginner's guide to advanced neurosurgery'

- *how-to guides and videos:* 'Step-by-step guide to building a rabbit hutch'

- *reviews:* 'The top 100 films you never want to see'

- *expert interviews:* 'In-depth interviews with sacked footy coaches: why they can't let go'

- *lists of resources:* 'Sam Kekovich's pocket guide to vegan restaurants in North Queensland'

- *case studies and examples:* 'How I lost 50 kg in 30 days on the Oxygen Diet'

- *insider information:* 'How to win a medal at the Olympics without even trying' by Steve Bradbury

- *timely news and alerts:* 'Financial planning for octogenarians: it's never too late to start'.

Darren Rowse on how to monetise a blog

Darren Rowse knows a thing or two about creating information products.

As a lover of cameras and writing, he decided to merge his interests and blog about cameras, and now he gets paid to do it. Genius! That was back in 2004 and he has since gone on to become one of the world's leading bloggers and blogger coaches.

His blogs are read by more than five million people each week so he knows what he's talking about, and he's been a full-time blogger for more than a decade. I wanted to know his secrets to monetising blogs. I've heard it's very simple:

- You wake up.

- You write a bit.

- You post it.

- You go out for lunch.

- You come back.

- You check your bank account.

- You're richer now than before you left.

Let's put that little fantasy to bed and discover exactly how Darren got started.

Bernadette: How did you get started as a blogger?

Darren: I was reviewing cameras and giving photography tips and it really caught on because it was at the time when cameras started to be incorporated into mobile phones, so interest in cameras exploded. It was a lot of good luck and timing.

I saw people starting to use blogs a while back to build their profile, but they weren't directly monetising them and yet other websites were being monetised, so I could see where it was heading. I think most people knew that eventually blogs would become commercial, but we didn't really have the tools to do it. I was surprised that there was controversy about it, but I was also surprised how quickly the industry developed. Things like ad networks and blogging conferences started to pop up really quickly, which was a big surprise.

Bernadette: How did you make money from your blog in the early days?

Darren: I made money in 2004 through Google's AdSense Network. The attraction for me was that it was really easy to use. It was just a matter of putting a little bit of code in your side bar or in your template and it would suddenly serve up ads to readers of my blog and I would make money every time someone clicked on the ads.

Bernadette: *How much did you earn?*

Darren: On a good day I was earning a few dollars a day. That's when I had a few thousand readers. It wasn't really that much at all but if you think about that seven days a week, 365 days a year, it adds up.

Bernadette: *Who was paying you?*

Darren: On the Digital Photography School blog, a lot of advertisers targeted our site because they knew we were a decent brand. When that happens and they want to align with your brand, that pushes the prices up of what they are willing to pay. You can earn thousands of dollars a month with it, but you need millions of readers to get to that sort of level.

Bernadette: *What about now? How do you earn money?*

Darren: The main way I make money now is through online information. In the past five years we have created 34 eBooks. Some of the early eBooks were based on content we had already written on the blog and we compiled it together into a PDF, but the next 32 eBooks have all been original content. We work with authors to write those and then do a revenue share agreement with the authors.

(I can hear your ears prick up about now, so yes, I'll ask.)

Bernadette: *How does someone go about becoming an author for you?*

Darren: We would want to know that someone is an expert in their field. So if they are writing about photography, they would need to be a photographer and know what they are doing and be able to teach well and work well within my team.

Bernadette: *Who's in your team?*

Darren: We have a producer, a designer, proofreaders and a marketing team. It takes three or four months to get them from whoa to go, so they have got to work well with that team and hit the deadlines as well.

We quite often work with the same authors multiple times and develop about three or four books so that we can buy all of them together from that one author.

Affiliate marketing explained

Bernadette: What if I don't want to make a product? Can I make money referring other people's products?

Darren: Yes. That's called affiliate marketing. This is when you get paid a commission to recommend a product. Or it's when you send someone to a website and they buy the product based on clicking that link and then you earn a commission on that.

Bernadette: What was your first experience with affiliate marketing?

Darren: The first program I ever joined was Amazon's affiliate program, which they called their Associates Program. We recommended books. I was earning around 4 per cent commission per book, which isn't very much at all, but some pay up to 8 per cent.

But over time, if you are recommending a lot of books and then you get into recommending cameras, like we did, it all adds up. And then if you send somebody into Amazon and they go out and buy something else like a ride on lawn mower that is worth something around $20 000 or $30 000 then that generates a good commission. And when you are sending people to have a look at a camera, they can go on to buy all kinds of stuff and it becomes very lucrative.

> **Tip**
> Affiliate marketing is when you get paid a commission to recommend a product.

Bernadette: Could I make money by recommending your information products?

Darren: Yes. Anyone can. For example, if you recommended someone buy an eBook from us you could get up to 40 per cent commission, so on a bundle of eBooks worth $100, you'd make $40 commission. It can add up quite quickly.

Bernadette: Do you need a large database to make a lot of money as an affiliate?

Darren: Those who do well may not have a large audience, but they have a solid, trusted relationship with that audience. And it's important that you recommend high-quality products that really, really relate to the topic that you are writing about.

Bernadette: Can you recommend any affiliate programs for people to explore?

Darren: A lot of retail outlets in Australia have what's called affiliate networks. Rakuten (www.rakuten.com) is one of those and they represent different retail stores and operate under the same type of principle in that you send people to their sites through your link and you earn a commission. There's also CJ Affiliate by Conversant (www.cj.com) and clixGalore (www.clixgalore.com.au).

If you want to make serious money online, build a bridge

If you've ever been to Sydney, you'll know you have to pay a toll to get from the north of Sydney into the city, and vice versa.

Now think of all the traffic that crosses the bridge in any day. That's a lot of cars. So it's fair to say that whoever collects the toll is making a pretty penny. Did they build the bridge? No. Do they own the cars? No. So what do they own? Nothing! But they own the rights to that bridge so no matter who crosses it, they get a clip of the ticket.

Great business model, hey? Just as long as they maintain the bridge, and make sure that the traffic flows nicely and that there are no accidents or hold-ups on the bridge, everyone is happy.

So how does this relate to making money online? Using the bridge analogy, have a think about how you could connect buyers and sellers of some product or service and take a 'clip' of the 'ticket' each time they go through. You don't need to sell, buy or stock anything; you just need to introduce people who need something from each other.

Here are some examples of very famous, very successful 'bridge-builder' sites (or brokerages):

- www.freelancer.com

- www.odesk.com

- www.elance.com

- www.etsy.com

- www.ebay.com

- www.gumtree.com.au

- www.wotif.com

- www.carsales.com.au

There's also a similar but different style of site, called a 'price comparison' site, which lists all the various competitors in a sector, say in the energy, health insurance or telco world. They make all the products, prices and features available for viewing and then take a cut of whichever products or services are purchased from the site. Again, they don't own the products or services; they just connect the buyer with the seller.

> **Tip**
>
> If you want to make serious money online, build a bridge.

Spoiler alert! To make a business like this work, you need extremely deep pockets to promote it. Its success rests on generating traffic and that costs money. Big money. And the model is very susceptible to competition because the barriers to entry are low. Anyone, given enough money and access to the right players, could set up an alternative 'bridge'. What if they build one right next to yours?

Matt Barrie is one of the most successful 'bridge builders' Australia has produced and is the founder of Freelancer, one of the world's largest outsourcing marketplaces.

Q & A with Matt Barrie on how to make money online

Freelancer is the ultimate disruptive site. Its founder, Matt Barrie, gives his tip on other industries that are ripe for disruption and what kids should be studying to future-proof their earning potential.

Bernadette: Which businesses are ripe for disruption?

Matt: Just walk down the street and see any business that's got a lot of people involved, and it's ripe for disruption. Why? Because people are quite inefficient. They make errors. Software doesn't, and it's quite cost-effective. You can go and find databases and web servers and graphic design packages for free. Email is free and Skype is mostly free. And what's not free is cheap—like cloud computing, or buying domain names. So people are literally financing businesses off the back of a credit card.

Bernadette: Any examples of an industry that might be ripe for disruption?

Matt: Real estate is a classic example. It's a tremendously inefficient business—in every single suburb in the country you see not one, but six or more real estate agents in a row with the most expensive property in every suburb advertised using these little bits of cardboard in the window. We don't search for property by looking through the window anymore. We do it online.

So these inefficient industries are everywhere. And now, thanks to Open Source, a lot of the software you need to build this type of business is actually free.

Future-proofing our kids

Bernadette: What should our children be studying to set them up for a successful career?

Matt: It's really critical that people get out there and pursue degrees in science, technology, engineering and mathematics,

(continued)

105

Q & A with Matt Barrie on how to make money online (cont'd)

which is basically STEM, because this nation is a pretty primitive colony where we basically just dig stuff out of the ground, put it on the boat and ship it overseas without elaborately transforming it into manufactured goods anymore.

You have to get to them early because by Year 10 they've already figured out what they're going to do with their career. So my advice for high-school students is get into technology. The days of being average are over. And it's an amazing industry to get into—we're talking everything from satellites to Google glasses, mobile phones and driverless cars.

Pricing for profit

Generally speaking, price is a function of everything it costs to make a product, plus a mark-up on top to generate a profit, and that's it.

Or is it?

Consider the luxury-goods industry, a triumph of capitalism over common sense.

- *Jewellery.* Ounce for ounce, does a Tiffany gold necklace cost more to produce than a gold necklace made by Pandora? No.

- *Christian Louboutin shoes.* Using the exact same materials, stitching and craftsmanship, does it cost more to produce a Louboutin shoe than one made by Nine West? No.

- *Ralph Lauren.* Using the exact same materials, stitching and craftsmanship, does it cost more to produce a Polo shirt than one made by Bonds? No.

What these luxury brands do so brilliantly is use their logo to elevate the product above all others in the market, and then use an inflated price to anchor that perception of quality in the mind of the consumer. Without the red soles, would anyone really know the shoes were from Louboutin? Without the little polo-player icon, would anyone really know the shirt was from Ralph Lauren?

The answer is almost certainly no.

It's these identifiable symbols that give the product its luxury status, but the price is a key element in that.

Here's proof. You see a Tiffany necklace on eBay for $99. Your first thought is: 'It must be a fake' or 'Her marriage busted up and she's liquidating her assets'. For the sisterhood, let's hope it's the former.

The same goes for any other luxury or high-value service: if it's priced too cheaply and is not congruent with our perception of what the price should be, we instantly think it must be fake, second-hand or damaged. Imagine if Warren Buffett or Tony Robbins priced their one-to-one mentoring services at $60 per hour? What if Harvard University offered a three-year degree for $5000 per year? We'd instantly be thinking, 'What's the catch?'

And it's interesting to note that luxury brands rarely have sales or end-of-season clearances. To do so would not just discount their profit margins but their image also.

So what does this have to do with online marketing? Well, everything.

Here's the thing. In the absence of being able to touch, sense and experience your online product, and without a luxury logo to anchor its prestige in our minds, we have to use other techniques to reinforce the product's quality: the website, the graphics, the copy, the reputation of the owner of the site, and of course, pricing.

Do I have to be the cheapest to succeed online?

Those selling online products and services that aren't luxury brands or high-value services often think they have to be the cheapest to compete. But this is not necessarily so.

One person who knows a lot about online pricing is Paul Greenberg, founder of Deals Direct, Australia's first online department store. He's sold millions of products online so I was curious to get his opinion about price. I wanted to ask him the questions I get asked all the time, which are:

Bernadette: How can we possibly compete with the likes of the impossibly cheap products coming out of China?

Paul: Competition on price is often referred to by the industry as a race to the bottom; it's not a sustainable model. But competitive pricing is the new world, so we need to get used to it. Lazy pricing in the new borderless retail is long behind us.

Bernadette: What is the difference between value and price?

Paul: We surveyed tens of thousands of our customers at Deals Direct and they always said that they preferred the term 'value' to 'price', and that in their minds, there was a distinct difference.

'Value' is a broad basket of customer benefits that includes convenience like the home-delivery model, as well as the post- and pre-sale service.

Tim Davies, seller and education manager for eBay, discovered some interesting insights about price when he researched a group of eBay buyers.

Tim: Interestingly, several of them told us that they didn't mind paying a higher price online compared to what they would pay in an offline retail store.

Bernadette: Why would they be happy to pay more to shop online? Shouldn't it be cheaper?

Tim: They said, 'We know we have to pay for petrol, we have to find a park and maybe pay for that. We have to leave home, battle the traffic and negotiate the crowds, so we're happy to pay a bit extra for the convenience of being able to shop from home'.

Bernadette: So it's not just about the price?

Tim: What online retailers have to understand is that it's not just who's got the cheapest price. The customer is evaluating a whole range of things which make up 'value' for a person. Value means different things to different people.

'The pricing rule of 3': how to use pricing to your advantage

For online entrepreneurs tempted to cut prices to remain competitive, here's a clever pricing strategy that helps you target more customers, stops them comparing you to the competitors, and generates more revenue too.

Price wars are a pain in the neck for everyone except the buyer. And if you don't have deep pockets and can't sustain the price cutting, you'll be the only one who loses out.

> What online retailers have to understand is that it's not just who's got the cheapest price.
>
> **Tim Davies**

So, wouldn't it be great if you could keep your price higher than the competition while actually increasing sales?

By using 'the pricing rule of 3', you can turn your competitors' lower prices into an advantage for you. Here's how it works.

'The pricing rule of 3'

It's no secret that if two products are identical in all respects, people will generally buy the one that costs less. However, research has consistently proven that if buyers are exposed to a third product that costs more than either of the original two, people will usually pick the mid-priced product rather than the cheapest one.

By 'anchoring' the mid-range price point as the standard price, everything more expensive than that will seem 'too expensive', and conversely, everything cheaper than that is, well, cheaper. Less than. Not quite right. For the cheapskates...you get the drift.

Create a third price point

Here's a practical example of how you could do this.

Let's suppose you're selling a service for $2000 that's similar to a service that your competitor is selling for $1500. You *could* offer your service for $1000, but that's just playing the price-war game and the only one losing is you.

Instead, offer three versions of your service:

- Product A: $1000

- Product B: $1500

- Product C: $2000.

The three services don't have to be wildly different as long as you label them appropriately. Most companies use terms like Gold, Silver and Bronze; or Deluxe, Premium and Standard to make it easy for customers to understand.

This way, you have a product for all price points and when a customer says they 'can't afford $2000' you can easily direct them to the lower priced products and still retain their custom.

Most people will pick the mid-priced point so make sure that this is the package that is of most value to your audience and generates most profit for you. If they like that product, chances are they'll upgrade to the higher package when they need more of what you have to offer.

Product for prospect

You can also provide a much cheaper price point, even a free product, that you can use as a lead generator to introduce customers to you, your product and your company.

This three-tiered pricing structure is known as the ascension model.

You see lots of companies offering free seminars who upsell you while you're at the seminar to a one-day course for $997 and then upsell you at the next seminar for a three-day course for $2997, and so on. It's a successful way of marketing a high-end product and it can be used for all sorts of products and services.

Most people want the best product and don't mind paying for it. By taking price off the table as a factor and showing customers the range of services you have at different price points, you're more likely to gain a customer at a price point that suits them and you.

Here are a few examples (see table 4.3) of how different businesses can use the three-step pricing model to capture as many new customers as possible

Table 4.3: examples of the three-step pricing model

Business	Pricing model
Spa and beauty salon	Express facial = $30 Standard facial = $75 Deluxe facial = $120
Coaching program	Entry level 60-minute webinar package = $97 Intermediate 5-hour webinar package = $497 Premium both of the above + a 2-hour private coaching session = $997
Children's book illustrator	Bronze package: unlimited 'how to draw' videos = free Silver package: 5 × autographed 'how to draw' books = $49 Gold package: both of the above + online access to live tutorials = $97

Measure twice, cut once

There were few topics about which all the entrepreneurs agreed, but there was one about which everyone did, and that was the need to measure everything, and I mean *everything*.

As H. James Harrington famously said, 'if you can't measure it, you can't manage it.'

Maximising profit is being able to know what works in your business and what doesn't. By applying sophisticated tracking tools and measurements to virtually every aspect of the business, anyone can learn to amplify the factors that increase it and eliminate the factors that don't.

> We measure everything.
>
> Matt Barrie

Some would say that it's this democratisation of data and analytics that has enabled the smaller, nimble players to outfox the bigger, more well-resourced players, because when you know where every marketing dollar goes and whether it's working or not, you can achieve incredible results on a very small budget.

Prior to Google Analytics, it was virtually impossible to accurately track buyer behaviour or determine how or why someone bought from your site. Now, everything is measurable and this measurability has been a game-changer. Google Analytics is the tool of choice for most of the entrepreneurs, and irrespective of whether they sell products or services they all use this free tool, or something similar to it.

Matt Barrie (co-founder of Freelancer) is meticulous with analytics.

> We measure everything. We measure the success of these things with revenue. It's all about growth. We have thousands of graphs that we monitor in real time on our site because everything has a funnel. Every funnel has conversion ratios all the way through and ultimately it leads to revenue or sign-ups or some other key driver in the business. And for us the key drivers are revenue, users and projects.

If you receive a book from Tony Nash's Booktopia and it's crushed or dented, Tony's tracking systems can tell you who packed the book, on what day and at what time.

Jodie Fox wishes she'd started measuring earlier.

> In hindsight, we should have been more sophisticated with our reporting because it gives us so much information that better informs our decisions. It's about understanding the funnels, which are of critical importance, but you should also be looking at the metrics across the entire business.

What would Jodie have measured differently if she was starting over?

I would have focused more heavily on customer acquisition costs, conversion rates, the lifetime value of customers, basket size, our burn rate (how much cash the business has) and revenue versus growth.

I was curious as to what Stephanie Alexander measured.

I look at my sales figures every day and that tells me where the sales are being generated, which is overwhelmingly in Australia. I also keep an eye on the response to social media when we put a post on my Facebook business page or an Instagram image. Sometimes you can see that there is a great response to that particular theme and I take note of that. I am not sure what it is actually telling me except that a lot of people liked it.

John Winning, founder of Appliances Online, could reel off his units of measurements without blinking.

The top-level KPIs I look for would be revenue, profit, gross margin, and obviously, cash flow. From a marketing perspective, there's the cost per acquisition, what channels you are getting your traffic from, what is your word of mouth, your 'Net Promoter Scores' and customer experience.

But wait, John's got more.

If it's for the warehouse, then you'd be looking at how many movements you are doing between receiving and delivery and trying to become as efficient as possible. Technology-wise, I'd be looking for how many bugs are popping up versus how many jobs you are able to complete and in what type of time frames. There's a million KPIs.

ProBlogger's Darren Rowse measures other factors.

We also look at comment levels and how many people are sharing content. We also look out for questions we get via email about a particular new product or a new trend in photography. We just constantly listen for that type of thing and we also watch what other people are doing and how well their promotions seem to be going on their products.

Tip

If you can measure it, you can improve it.

Brad Smith was the 2010 Young Australian of the Year for Tasmania. He's a champion Superlite MX motocross rider and founder of the very successful braaap motorcycle and accessories retail outlet he calls 'the motocross equivalent of a surf shop'.

He's packed a lot into his short life and one of the reasons he believes he's been successful is because he's been able to measure what works and what doesn't.

> I know I have at least eight 'points of contact' with a prospect before they'll buy something from me. We track those contact points and can pinpoint with laser accuracy when the prospect will buy.

He has also developed a range of activities and marketing initiatives to maximise those contact points, so instead of having his sales team ringing prospects just to 'see how they're going', he offered them something he knows will drive sales. For example, he created a

Tip

Increase your customer touch points and you'll increase your sales.

motorcycle riding school because he knows that once a prospect has personally experienced the thrill of a great ride—with top instructors, powerful bikes and first-class equipment—they'll want to buy the bike, or at least take some lessons (and the lessons are just another 'contact point'), moving them another step along the road to a purchase. Genius.

Working with investors

If you've got world domination in your sights, you'll want to know how to find, work with and get the most out of investors.

Online entrepreneurs take on investment partners for all sorts of different reasons. Sometimes it works brilliantly, other times it can take you off track.

When Andre Eikmeier, co-founder of the online wine retailer Vinomofo, found himself courted by an investment 'suitor', he discovered it was a bit of both.

Bernadette: How did your investment partnership journey begin?

Andre: About 20 months after launching Vinomofo we came on the radar of a big retail operator and the big traditional distributors in the supply chain model. They didn't like the idea of an independent player that was doing things aggressively with price. They said we were 'disrupting the supply chain model'.

Bernadette: What did they do to you?

Andre: They straight away started putting pressure on suppliers on what they should do with us, and we realised that this could wind up our business very quickly.

Bernadette: What did you do?

Andre: We needed to get investors in so that we could scale up and get some big buying power quickly. We were only ordering 20 cases of wine at a time so we were a small player by comparison, and our suppliers were taking a big risk with their larger distributors by placing our order of 20 cases.

Bernadette: What happened then?

Andre: We spoke to a large media player about investment, but in the end we got approached by Catch of the Day, a big online retail group, an agile, aggressive company who have done extraordinary things.

We went with them because they had proven that they could be category leaders in a few businesses that they had launched. So we sold a majority stake of the company to them and joined their group but we operated quite independently.

Bernadette: What were the advantages in doing that?

Andre: We tapped into their audience and their media, so transactions suddenly boomed and we really grew quite aggressively. It gave us the buying power that we needed and that surprised all those serious players. As a result, our suppliers started kicking back on pressure from the retail giants.

Bernadette: How did that change things for you?

Andre: Well, now we could put in an order of 2000 cases instead of 20 cases. We also had really good payment terms that weren't the norm in the industry. But then we ended up buying that stake back a little while later. I think we really found that the industry and our customers and everybody thought we are an underdog and we needed to follow that journey, which is why we bought the company back.

Bernadette: What were the drawbacks of going out on your own again without the support of a major online retailer like that?

> On the first day of our new arrangement, without their backup, we had zero in the bank account.
>
> Andre Eikmeier

Andre: Venturing with a big partner like Catch of the Day enabled us to have an effectively limitless bank account so there was a safety net, which is good and bad. It's good because it allows you to make more aggressive decisions if you need to buy large volumes of stock. But it also frustrated us a little bit about the business because it became a bit about 'the Tuesday mornings sales report' and being part of that bigger structure did take away that sort of connection we had with our audience.

Bernadette: Was it hard starting over?

Andre: On the first day of our new arrangement, without their backup, we had zero in the bank account. But then at 12:01 am the first sale came through and that was good because we had seven days to pay! So it was really visceral again and it really charged us up.

Bernadette: Having seen it from both sides, what would you prefer? Having the security of a big player supporting you or being able to run fast and free?

Andre: The challenge was to get profitable quickly again because there was no safety net, but I think we liked it because it focused our decisions and it allowed us to think bigger picture in the longer term, knowing we weren't headed towards an exit or an IPO or any other artificial agenda. It enabled us to make pure business decisions.

Jodie Fox, co-founder of the online design-your-own-shoes shop Shoes of Prey, has an eight-step strategy for sourcing investors.

The 8-step beginner's guide to sourcing investors

1. Firstly, decide if you want, need or have to have investors, and be categorically certain what you will give up for their involvement and what you want in return.

2. Next, you need to get a warm introduction, so you need to know what you want to get out of your business and then you need to have a look at the venture capital funds or angel investors who are interested in investing in your area. This warm introduction is very important because you can send cold-call emails as often as you want, but these guys get so many cold emails every single day that it's impossible to get cut-through.

3. Your first meeting should never be about closing the deal. It should be like your first date: get to know each other a little bit, share a bit of information and agree to have another conversation. You want to inspire them a bit about what you are doing and help them to get to know what is great about you as a person and your own team.

4. You need to consider whether you want just money or smart money. Smart money is investors and board members who will contribute to the business in terms of expertise or a network you can tap into for hiring. It's important to think about what else you want besides money, before you seek out investors.

(continued)

The 8-step beginner's guide to sourcing investors (cont'd)

5. After the warm introduction—that is, the first 'date'—the second meeting, or second 'date', should be a more detailed conversation about exactly what the company is doing and if all goes well, start looking at the next steps.

6. If they are interested they will take your proposal to their partner meeting. If the partners show interest then you go into the terms and conditions surrounding how much money will be given.

7. The term sheet is all those conditions on which you had agreed that the money would come into your business. After the term sheets are given, you go into the due diligence phase, where they have access to everything in the company and go through all of your financials. They might want to sit down with certain people in your company as well.

8. If that all goes well then you do the legal paperwork. Once that's completed and signed off you will have money in your account and you are off!

Simple!

Jodie also recommends keeping these seven tips in mind when seeking investors.

7 helpful tips to keep in mind when seeking investors

1. Fundraising always takes longer than you think it will.

2. If you're selling an unusual concept, like we were in the form of bespoke shoes, you have to appreciate that you're asking

people to part with their hard-earned cash, and it can take a long time to get people to come along with you.

3. Investors are not just investing in the ideas, they're investing in you, and what they're looking for is a really strong team: people who can execute the idea. Good ideas are everywhere but the real question is, can the good idea be executed? That is what they are really looking for.

4. Don't have the investor conversations until you're ready to raise money. We spent too much time on exploratory conversations when we weren't really ready to take on investors and we wasted a lot of time.

5. When taking cash on board, think about what you are promising your shareholders and really ask yourself, can you achieve those things you're promising? You need an exact view of what you can do, how much money you need and how you're going to spend that money.

6. Be clear about why you want investor funding. We took on funding because we wanted the business to grow faster and everything required more capital. We didn't take a salary for the first two and a half years.

7. You should reward the people who are taking a chance on you and giving you cash. Giving meaningful equity at the start of the business should reward their risk-taking. Remember that in the beginning any percentage of nothing is still nothing. I'd rather have a small slice of a big pie than a big slice of nothing.

Making money from your business is the reason you're in business, so be sure to look ahead to the future, see what the trends are going to be and get yourself set up to take advantage of the next wave of industry disruption.

Maximising profit is the name of the game in business, so this chapter should have given you some ideas on how to choose the right business model for you. There's enormous opportunity to make money in the marketplace for anyone with a niche product or service and an equally niche audience. You just have to work out how you're going to make money from it.

We've covered a range of different business models and the various merits of each. All work brilliantly, but you have to be mindful of the investment required to bring them to life. This all comes back to the original question: What do you want? So if you still haven't clarified that, it will be hard to pinpoint the right model for you.

Working with investors can be a brilliant launch pad to world domination, or it can severely restrict your style and vision.

Get clear on what you want from investors before you seek them out, and be very clear about what you'll give up in order to get them.

What's next?

In chapter 5, we'll cover one of the most important factors for any online entrepreneur wanting to build a business that works: trust. What it is, why it matters, how to get it and how it can have a massive impact on your profit.

CHAPTER FIVE
POSITIONING

> Trust everybody, but cut the cards.
>
> *Finley Peter Dunne*

The trust quotient: would you buy from you?

When dining at restaurants, my 75-year-old dad used to follow the waiter to the cash register to check they didn't copy down the number of his credit card.

'Dad, this is a reputable restaurant! Look, they have tablecloths and everything!'

'Bernadette, you can never be too careful,' he'd say.

He was of that old-school generation that didn't, and still doesn't, trust online transactions. Was he paranoid? A bit. Was I embarrassed watching Dad follow the waiter to the cash register? A lot. But was he right to be cautious? Yes. He's on the far end of the spectrum in terms of lack of trust. I'm probably too far the other way.

But he represents what most people fear when they give their credit-card details over the internet. And that is, 'Can I trust them?'

The Zero Moment of Truth and how to influence it

One of the biggest reasons online businesses go under is because they fail to position their business as a trusted authority – to instil a sense of security in the buyer.

Think about it.

They've landed on your page. Big tick for you.

They want to buy your product. Another big tick.

But just as they're about to push the 'Buy' button, they stop. They pause, fingers hovering over the mouse. At that precise moment, which Google has termed the ZMOT (Zero Moment of Truth), your site's positioning – its credibility – is being weighed up. In the blink of an eye, everything they've ever heard, seen or experienced about your brand comes zooming into their brain like a tsunami and when it ebbs away, equally rapidly, it leaves its detritus: an impression, a feeling, that is staggering in its simplicity. It's either, 'Yes, we trust you' or 'No, we don't'.

Let's clarify what we're asking customers to do here: we're asking them to give us the most cherished piece of data they possess – their credit-card details – to a stranger 'in the cloud' in the hope that we are who we say we are. To people like my dad, it's akin to signing a blank cheque, giving it to a stranger and saying, 'Just fill in the missing bits and bank it'. It's no wonder some online businesses go under; they fail to realise the gravitas of what they are asking their customers to do at that final moment of purchase.

Think about your site from your customers' point of view. Objectively. Dispassionately. Would you buy from it? Would *you* trust you?

How to build trust and minimise risk

So the real question for all online entrepreneurs is, 'How can we build trust in our sites so that people from around the world (or just around the corner) feel comfortable buying from us?' The good news is there are lots of ways to achieve this. Most are inexpensive, within your control and can be achieved quite quickly.

Sure, as you'll discover, creating trust is all a bit of 'smoke and mirrors', but perception is everything in online business and although in isolation these strategies seem quite basic, the sum of each is much greater than the parts. Each piece becomes yet another brick in your 'wall of trust'.

On-page factors also have a massive impact on whether the shopper completes their purchase.

'More people abandon their purchase at the check-out page than at any other time on the site,' says Phil Leahy, founder of the online retailing industry's premiere event, Internet Conference (www.internetconference.com.au), and a former powerseller on eBay.

> It doesn't take much to put people off; a slow-loading page, onerous terms and conditions, a request to log in and create a password. All these reduce the credibility factor, and therefore the conversion rate, so these risk factors need to be either eliminated altogether or addressed before the shopper gets to the check-out page.

So how is this 'yes, we trust you/no, we don't' feeling created?

That's the province of consumer psychologists and cutting-edge behavioural science and although we'll truly never know what makes people buy what they do, there are proven strategies we can apply to our businesses that help increase the trust quotient and reduce the perceived risk of buying online.

What we do know for certain is that prior to the internet and social media, tracking the path to purchase and building trust was a whole lot easier.

Take a look at the limited number of touch points advertisers had to play with in the early 2000s to position a brand, build trust and drive sales:

- TV

- radio

- print (magazines)

- press (newspaper)

- PR

- direct mail

- direct sales.

Now compare this with the number of touch points advertisers have to play with now:

Facebook	Dropbox	Tumblr
Twitter	Skype	RSS
Pinterest	Vimeo	Picasa
Google+	Blogger	Flickr
LinkedIn	Reddit	Amazon
YouTube	ShareThis	and many more.

Is it any wonder recruitment agencies say the biggest demand for jobs is for data analysts? Anyone who can interpret the big data these sites throw up, and provide measureable insights about what's working and what's not, deserves the big bucks these jobs are paying.

Nine ways to increase your trust quotient

So how do you build trust and credibility for your online business? Believe it or not, you can manufacture trust. That sounds hypocritical, but it's not. All it means is that you don't have to wait for years to build a 'trusted' brand. There are practical steps you can take to build credibility for your company and in particular, your website, which will encourage people to entrust you with their credit card details.

Top 9 ways to build trust and credibility for your online business

These are the elements that help minimise the risk people often feel when buying something online from a new or little-known website:

- awards

- social media

- media exposure or PR

- contact details

- photos and product descriptions

- 'borrowing' other companies' logos

- testimonials

- customer service and refund policies

- money-back guarantees.

Let's have a look at each of these in detail.

The power of awards: $800 000 reasons to apply for them

One of the fastest ways to position your site as a trusted, credible business is to win, or even just apply for, an award.

I know a lot of offline entrepreneurs who steer clear of awards, averring them to be a 'waste of time', a 'wank', an 'ego-building' exercise. But almost every online entrepreneur I interviewed believed passionately in the value of business awards and how they can absolutely affect the bottom line.

In fact, you don't have to win, or even become a finalist, to reap the benefits of said awards. You just have to be nominated. Can you nominate yourself? Sure you can, or get a friend to do it for you. No-one has to know you nominated yourself. If you feel uncomfortable, get your mum to do it. Like I said, smoke and mirrors.

> **Tip**
>
> Apply for awards. They work. One carefully placed award logo generated $800000 for Booktopia.

I once nominated my friend for Australian of the Year. He didn't win, but now he can say on his website, 'Nominated for Australian of the Year'. Is it true? Yes. Does it help build trust? Sure does. Will it create a sale? Not necessarily. Awards and testimonials work best when the customer is ready to buy but just needs a little nudge in the right direction.

Tony Nash, co-founder of Booktopia, discovered that the placement of one award logo on his home page equated to an increase in revenue of more than $800000 in one year. And he's got the proof to back it up.

As an online retailer we need to do everything we can to reduce the perceived risk of buying from us. So when we won the Telstra Business Award we put the logo of the award on the top, right-hand side of our site. But we wanted to test it to see if the logo made any difference. It did. A big difference. We conducted split testing where one version of the home page (with the award logo) gets served up and then another version of the page (without the logo) gets served up. It's called A/B testing and it's super easy to do—all you need is a bit of code and you can test and measure a variety of elements.

… we wanted to test it to see if the logo made any difference. It did. A big difference.

Tony Nash

Well, after two weeks the results were clear. The page with the logo generated an extra 2 per cent in sales compared to the page without the logo. This may not sound like a lot, but on our turnover of $40 million, that translates to more than $800000 in sales in one year!

Not a bad return for putting a logo on your home page. Who says awards don't make a difference to the bottom line?

Kate Morris found awards immensely helpful in all sorts of ways. One of Kate's major challenges in getting her online business, Adore Beauty, off the ground was the unwillingness of major beauty brands to come on board as suppliers. But without the premium players, she knew her site would not cut it as the 'go to' site for the world's best brands.

> Awards really build credibility. Not just with your customers, but also with your strategic partners, so for us it was a big deal with the brands we wanted to work with. Certainly people do return your emails when you have the Telstra Business Women's Awards logo in your email signature! Personally, I am part of the Adore Beauty brand and we do use me a lot as the face of the brand, so as a brand-building exercise it was really important. It's great PR too.

Shoes of Prey's Jodie Fox had other reasons for applying for awards.

> They're important because, as an entrepreneur, you can lose sight of the successes you have along the way. Awards help you see what you're achieving and they help our team see their part in the success of the company. We have a team of 75 people around the globe and it's important for us to stop and say, 'Hey, you guys are doing an amazing job', because they are. It's pretty important to the culture of a team.

In addition to promoting your award on your site, you'll also get a big brownie point from Google if you win or get nominated. When I searched online for information on one of my interviewees, Simon Griffiths, founder of the online social enterprise Who Gives a Crap, the award sites mentioning him were often ranked higher than his own sites. This 'earned media' is the holy grail of trust and credibility. Simon didn't have to work too hard to prove his credibility. The award nomination did it for him.

Just apply: when one thing leads to another

I heard Christine Nixon speak at a conference about her experience leading a team of 14 000 police officers. She was asked, 'How did you land the top job of Chief Commissioner of Victoria Police?'

'I applied,' she said.

The fact is, most people don't apply for awards, which is exactly why you should. They think, 'I'll never win' or 'It's a waste of time' or 'How could I possibly beat so-and-so'. But you see, 'so-and-so' hardly ever applies either because they're thinking the same thing as you. Often it's people with over-inflated ideas of how good they are who actually do apply, yet those with genuine ability and credentials don't.

Awards beget awards

As Michael J. Fox once said about fame and the freebies that come with it: 'The more you've got, the more you get'.

He's quite right. Everyone knows that winning one award makes it easier to win the next one. Applying for an award when you've already won one is like sending in an invisible PR agent to give the judges a dazzling lightshow outlining why you are the best and why you should win. If all things are equal, and it comes down to you (who's won an award) and the other (who hasn't), odds are they're going to award the person who's already won the award. No-one, especially judges, likes to get things wrong and they'll tend to be swayed by what's gone before them when awarding prizes. The Halo Effect in action.

When we were renovating our kitchen, I entered a competition to win $6000 in kitchen appliances. All I had to do was write down in 25 words or less why I'd like an induction oven. I didn't even know what an induction oven was, but my 25-word poem ended with the word 'seduction'. (Yes, it was that kind of poem.) I won. So there. When the editor of the magazine rang to tell me I'd won, I asked, 'How many people other than me entered?' She said, 'None'.

Social media and why people don't trust advertising anymore

People often refer to social media as word-of-mouth on steroids. And they're right. How else can one post, one comment, one thought-bubble be transmitted to millions of people around the world in a millisecond? In 25 years of working in marketing, I have never seen anything as transformational as social media.

Everyone in the advertising agency game is feeling the heat. Why? Because advertising's once unchallenged power to shape public opinion and influence the purchase decision has been severely challenged. Yes, advertising is still relevant. Yes, it still works. But these days, you need a lot of green stuff to throw at it to make a ripple.

And in any case, for the thousands of 20-something-year-old start-up entrepreneurs working out of the spare room at their parents' house, finding a lazy $1 million to spend on a TV campaign to create awareness for their new killer app is just a tad outside their reach.

Fysh Rutherford, co-founder and creative director of the very successful t20 digital and social advertising agency, an elder statesman of the advertising industry and a funny, wise old geezer to boot, said this to me a while back.

Fysh: Bernie, when I write an advertisement for the paper, I have to be more thorough, more honest and more truthful than any other person in the communications game, including politicians, PR agents and promoters. It's a pain.

Bernadette: What do you mean, Fysh?

Fysh: Look at it this way. In PR and social media I can pretty much say what I like because it's a personal comment – an opinion – and no-one's going to go and fact-check a personal opinion. But an ad? Watch the competitors crawl all over it, looking for even a hint of untruth, a stretched idea, a glimmer of exaggeration. We have to be more careful with what we say, and be more exacting, than practically any other communications professional.

Note: Sure, the law around social media is catching up and owners of all social-media channels are responsible for the truth and accuracy of what comes up, but from what I can see, the watchdog that is the ACCC has yet to formulate and apply the tough consumer protection laws that all advertisers must adhere to in the mainstream media.

Does anyone even care about paid advertisements anymore?

Fysh has a point. With publicists creating sponsored content that seamlessly blends into the world of social media and subsequently gets passed off as fact; and with influential bloggers being paid to spruik a product through their channels ('cash for comment' repurposed, but without the obligation to disclose), does anyone even notice – let alone *care* about – the paid advertisement anymore, even if it is 100 per cent truthful and accurate?

Despite the army of lawyers nit-picking their way through the terms and conditions of Fysh Rutherford's advertisements, the reality is that social media provides a credibility foghorn that trumps advertising in all its forms. And it's showing no sign of stopping.

Here's a classic example of how social media comments (aka earned media) will always trump paid advertising.

A friend of mine, a social-media devotee, mentioned this story in passing one day over coffee, but it stuck with me.

Her washing machine had broken down. As any busy working mother of three would know, this is a major catastrophe. Without thinking, and certainly without rushing off to the nearest Good Guys outlet to make a purchase, she does what any self-respecting social-media junkie does: she jumps on Facebook and sends out a post saying, 'Help! My washing machine's died. Can anyone recommend where I can get another one urgently?'

Within seconds, because she's so unbelievably connected, she gets back a plethora of responses. 'Try Appliances Online. Good prices. They deliver, and they take away the old one for free.' Another post says the same thing, and another. Within three minutes she has all the information she needs to make a decision. Appliances Online it is.

> Not only does she go and buy from them, but she gets back online and praises Appliances Online to her tens of thousands of followers on Facebook and Twitter. Who needs advertising when you've got peer-to-peer endorsements like that?

No wonder Appliances Online spends a fraction on advertising compared to its competitors.

Why PR now works better than paid advertising

Harry M. Miller, the former theatrical agent and celebrity promoter always maintained: 'If you want to be famous, get your photo in the paper!'

Tip
Overheard at a café: 'It's in the papers; it must be true'.

Simple advice, and although it was dispensed to me more than 20 years ago, it still remains true.

Despite me bleating on about the demise of the printed metropolitan newspapers, there's no question their editorial content still holds enormous power to sway public opinion. Shock jocks and breakfast TV shows still use the papers as the number-one source of content for their shows, simply because they represent what most people consume as news that day, and we all know that shock jocks have the power to set the public agenda. So, the newspaper still matters.

Now that they're running on the smell of an oily rag, in some ways it should be easier to get your media release seen, especially if you write a good story and help the journalist find the angle. Here's how one positive news story in *The Age* newspaper helped sell out my copywriting courses for months on end.

A journalist rang me, wanting to write a story on how mothers could find creative ways to work from home. Having lots of mothers as copywriting students, I knew that the story would be more powerful coming from a student rather than me. So I put the journalist in touch with one of my star pupils, who had indeed created a thriving home-based copywriting business while caring for her children, and the story appeared a few weeks later. This was before social media, so who knows how far the story would have gone, but the following week I had more than 300 phone calls and emails enquiring about the copywriting course.

People poo-poo mainstream press and focus on social media, but nothing, in my opinion, is as effective in creating credibility as a positive news story in the mainstream press. This is why PR is a flourishing industry, pushed along, of course, by the thousands of retrenched journalists who've set up their own PR consultancies because no-one is reading the paper they used to write for. Now they get paid to create stories to pitch to the person they used to be who isn't there anymore. The irony!

The devil is in the detail: why contact details are so important

Tony Nash recalls the early days of Booktopia.

> The phone would ring. 'Hello, this is Tony from Booktopia. How can I help you?' They'd say, 'No, it's okay. I just wanted to see if you were real'. And they'd hang up!

People like to know there's someone behind the computer. That's so important, even these days when it's commonplace to buy online without needing to speak to a real person. I often find prospects of my copywriting course ring up just before they push the 'Buy' button to ask a final question, just to check if we're 'real'. For the most part, however, if you haven't convinced them of your credibility prior to that, they won't even bother contacting you via phone or email.

Phil Leahy, founder of The Internet Conference, explains it this way.

> Online business is about trust and you have to do everything you can to build up that sense of trust. You have to have a phone number on the site. You have to have a physical address or at least a PO box. You have to have an email address. You have to have lots of photos showing the product, and if you're a service, a photo of you, and if relevant, your staff. You have to have a generous returns policy. You have to have a money-back guarantee. These things all used to be 'optional'; in fact, lots of online retailers prided themselves on not providing any of these. Times have changed. Without these basic components, no-one will buy from you. And of course video is the best way to demonstrate your credibility.

Note: Beware, of course, that anyone at any time can look up your place of business on Google Maps. Only list your street address if it is safe to do so. Personal safety always trumps commercial considerations.

> **Tip**
> People like to know there's someone behind the computer.

Photos and product descriptions

Dean Ramler, co-founder of the online designer furniture company Milan Direct, invests heavily in 360-degree photography, for credibility reasons.

> We need to show people exactly what our products look like from every angle. And we are very particular and spend a lot of time writing great content that describes our products in detail.

Photography like that is not cheap, but Dean knows he's in the visual business and without accurate representations of what the product looks like, it can cause massive headaches for everyone: the customer, because it arrives and it's not what they want, and himself, because he has to manage a disgruntled customer and the return.

Brian Shanahan, co-founder of the homewares site Temple & Webster, concurs with Dean. His photography is lush and stylish, but it needs to be, he says.

> We're a shopping experience that inspires and excites through curation, strong visual styling and stunning photography. Online you can only shop with your eyes, and great imagery and editorial are everything.

Someone who isn't that concerned about 360-degree photography is Stephanie Alexander. I asked her how important photography was in showcasing the recipes for her Cook's Companion app. Thinking her answer would be 'very', I was surprised by her response.

> I think that for what we do, when the image will generally only be seen on a tablet or a mobile device, we needn't have invested in photography the way we did. It was expensive and I don't think, in hindsight, it was justified.

'Borrowing' other companies' logos: the fast-track method for building trust

Unlike millions of people around the world, I still read the newspaper. The hardcopy kind. Call me old fashioned but I still love it. The thud as it lands in a puddle on my front lawn; the challenge of unravelling the plastic wrap without tearing my hair out in frustration (am I the only one who struggles with this?); the thrill of discovering what treats the editor has curated for me. I occasionally check out breaking news online to get up-to-date feeds on topics of interest, but I really love the ritual of reading the paper, in bed, with my two slices of Vegemite toast and a steaming mug of hot coffee. Simple pleasures.

One morning, as I was spilling coffee and dropping crumbs onto the bed, I saw an advertisement for a course on 'how to massage your baby'. Apparently, you need a certificate to do it these days. As I read on, I noticed the course was endorsed by the Royal Children's Hospital (RCH). Hang on a tick! That sounds weird. Since when did the RCH endorse baby massage courses?

Hospitals rarely endorse things like that. 'Sounds a bit dodgy to me,' I thought.

So I looked closer and, as I expected, the RCH did not indeed endorse it. What the RCH is in fact doing is renting the venue to the course provider, like any hotel or function centre would, and the course organisers are using the hospital venue as a major selling point to add credibility to their offering. Nice one, baby massage people!

I'm not suggesting for a moment that this is unethical or illegal. In fact, I applaud the baby massage people for their lateral thinking. What they have successfully done by choosing this venue for their course is 'borrowed' the RCH brand to effectively 'endorse' their course, adding enormous credibility in the process.

Now, this strategy of 'borrowing' credibility can work for online and offline businesses, but it works particularly well with online businesses in the educational, medical, real estate and financial industries where credibility is everything and options to demonstrate that credibility are limited, especially if you're a start-up.

Leveraging others' logos

Many online companies 'borrow' credibility by posting on their home page the logos of the media institutions in which they have been featured: 'As seen in *The Age*, the *Financial Review*, *Christian Bikers Weekly*', and so on.

Others list the associations of which they are a member. One logo can have enormous power. Booktopia's Tony Nash recalls being asked by the Australian Booksellers Association (ABA) to become a member. Unable to establish any tangible benefit for being a member, clutching at straws, he asked, 'Do you have an 'ABA member' logo we can put on the site?' 'We don't have an ABA member logo,' they said. 'Can you design one?' Tony asked. 'Sure,' they said. And within weeks, Booktopia had the heretofore non-existent ABA logo on the site. Boom! Instant credibility.

Other associations, such as Master Builders Australia (MBA), CPA Australia and the Financial Planning Association of Australia (FPA), have all had great success in positioning their associations in such a way that being a member is a statement to the public that they are dealing with a reputable professional.

Logos of every persuasion – be they an association, a charity you sponsor, a media company you've worked with or an award you've won – convey instant credibility and should be sought and displayed whenever possible.

I saw a memory course use this 'borrowed' credibility technique very successfully for years. The organisers hired a function room at the University of Melbourne to run their course and plastered their advertising with 'Melbourne University presents...' Not strictly true, but they got away with it. And the course continues to run.

Here are a few examples from other industries of how you can 'borrow' credibility to promote your goods and services:

- an acting school holds its classes at a famous film studio

- a fashion company gets a concession shop within a major department store

- a financial-planning seminar holds its event in a bank building

- a laser rejuvenation clinic holds its event at a hospital

- a cooking school holds its class in a 5-star restaurant kitchen.

Getting people to buy from you for the first time will always be the hardest part. Take every opportunity you can to use association and award logos to boost your credibility and minimise risk.

The power of testimonials: I'll have what she's having

'Getting testimonials from existing customers is one of the easiest and most effective ways to build trust,' says Mark Middo, author of *5 Minute Business.*

Bernadette: So how do you get testimonials?

Mark: It's quite simple. By asking for them.

Massive tip. Thanks Mark. But he did have more to add.

You'd be surprised how many times people let really happy, satisfied customers go without asking them for a testimonial. Sure, it's confronting to ask someone what they think about you, but once you get over that initial fear, and you get a glowing testimonial, that one testimonial could mean the difference between a future sale and a non-sale. It's worth overcoming the fear to ask for it.

Bernadette: But what if you can't get over that fear, Mark? What if you're just not sure if they like you or not?' I asked.

Mark: If you're uncomfortable asking in person, email them a survey after the transaction and ask for it then, or if you're really cowardly, ask for it via LinkedIn. If you're seriously shy, ask your administrative assistant (my tip: if you don't have a PA, ask your mum!) to send the email so that you don't have to have any contact with them at all. The wording might be: 'Hi John, I was hoping that you might be able to jot down a few words outlining your recent experience with the company. Would that be okay with you? If so, the areas I'd like you to cover include our customer service, our responsiveness and the quality of our content...'

Bernadette: Is this the coward's way out of getting a testimonial?

Mark: Overcoming the fear to ask for testimonials is a small price to pay for the long-term value and revenue they can generate for your business.

If you have the chance, film the testimonial. Everyone knows you can fake a written testimonial, but videoed testimonials are hard to manufacture. They demonstrate in real time, in people's own voices the value that you offer.

How to source a testimonial that works

Having sourced both written testimonials for my business and filmed testimonials for clients, there are a couple of tricks I've found to be very helpful when sourcing great testimonials that have a real impact.

Firstly, it helps to know what you want people to say about you. So, jot down a few rough notes of the things you want people to say and then write down the questions that will most likely elicit that answer. 'Leading the witness', I think it's called.

Let's say you want them to nominate the thing they liked most about the course or event they just attended. Here are a few questions you can ask (and some mock answers) that will deliver great results.

Q: What was the *best* thing about this course?

(They can't help but re-phrase the question as they're still processing the question while they answer it—and note that we don't ask, 'What did you think of the course?' or 'Did you like the course?' No. We ask specific questions that encourage them to paraphrase the question in the answer so that their response looks natural and fluid.)

A: The best thing about the course was the food! I stuffed myself silly and no-one said a thing. I even pocketed a few pastries to eat on the train home. The staff were so accommodating, they even offered me extra napkins so the jam wouldn't get stuck to the fluff in my coat pocket.

Q: Would you *recommend* the course to others, and if so, why?

A: I would definitely recommend the course to others because where else do you get paid to sit at the back of a room and play Candy Crush and check Facebook.

Q: What would you say to people considering enrolling in the course and why?

A: I would say to people, 'Just do it!'

Q: Why?

A: Because they didn't ask those stupid questions at the end like 'What did you learn?' and 'What will you take back to the office?' and embarrass me, so for those reasons, yeah, I'd really recommend it.

If they don't naturally paraphrase back the key words (which most do), ask them to repeat the question in their answer. Works a treat.

If you ask the right questions, testimonials practically write themselves.

Enough about me. What do you think of me?

If you've got a spare $50000 to invest in qualitative market research, you can discover what other people think and feel about you and your brand. If you don't, I have a really quick and dirty process that helps you work it out. It's not scientific, but it's pretty accurate. It's called the personal branding audit and it's featured in chapter 6. But a warning: man up. It may not be pretty.

The dented tin syndrome: the psychology behind testimonials

I'm not a psychologist, but having taught consumer behaviour regularly over the years at various universities, I have extensively researched the process of buying, and as a copywriter, I understand that the 'path to purchase' is at the core of every piece of copy I write.

But mainly, I've just been very observant of my own reactions during the buying process. For example, I notice the way my eye travels when I shop at the supermarket.

Firstly, I tend to ignore the products on the higher shelves. 'Must be discontinued,' I think, relegating perfectly good brands to the status of 'outliers', simply because they're on the top shelf. (And this is coming from someone who knows that companies pay vast sums to the supermarket giants for those facings (shelves) at eye level).

Secondly, I hardly ever buy the last tin of tuna on the shelf. 'Must be past its use-by date,' I say to myself.

And lastly, I never buy a tin that's dented, as if a knock has tainted its contents. Bizarre, hey?

So, when we don't have any of these visual marketing cues that buying offline provides us with, how can we as online sellers create a sense of trust for our online customers? How can we position our product as the best one to meet their needs?

Unlike the supermarkets, which cleverly lead us by the nose to choose the product of their choice, a search result on page one of Google does no such thing. Other than ranking one page over another (which admittedly is very important) once we're off Google and down on the ground, comparing site to site, it's up to us to determine which company, product or service is best for us. Assuming everything else is the same – price, product, quality, service, offer, terms – then the only thing consumers can turn to is what others say about us.

That's when the power of testimonials kicks in. Like awards, they won't make someone buy something they have no interest in, but they could be just the thing that tips them into choosing our product over another.

When the best service is no customer service at all

In the early days of online business (which wasn't that long ago), people were attracted to internet endeavours because it gave them a chance to (a) work from home (a big attraction for introverts) and (b) not speak to anyone (a big attraction for socially awkward types with strange obsessions with their mother and/or cats).

As such, technology enabled them to have the freedom to be themselves and still make money without having to engage with the outside world. Hurrah. Happy days.

The trouble was, this aversion to any contact extended to their customer-service policy too.

Call me old fashioned, but when I buy something and it breaks, or doesn't work, or is just a plain rip-off, I tend to want to speak to someone about getting it fixed. But could you get in touch with these people after the sale? Forget it. No email address. No street address. No phone number. No nothing. Try getting a response, let alone a refund! It was enough to make you cry. And on more than one occasion I did, as I got ripped off yet again with a dodgy American educational product that promised the world but delivered a pathetic PDF file. And it was one of the reasons Australians took their time becoming comfortable with online shopping. It was just too damn risky!

> I always say the best service is no service at all.
>
> Shaun O'Brien

But now? Oh, how the tides have turned. Australian online retailers are setting the standard for customer service everywhere.

Shaun O'Brien, founder of the online eBay store Selby Acoustics is one of them.

> Certainly six or seven years ago, everyone was getting online because they didn't want to deal with the customer. But now, you have to embrace customer service as an opportunity, whether it be a complaint or just an enquiry. My opinion on service is you need to do everything that you would do to a person if they were standing in front of you, but you've got to do it better because it's harder to communicate, especially as emails can get taken out of context.
>
> I always say the best service is no service at all. A customer should be able to go onto the site, find out the information they want, order the product, get what they want quickly and have no problem with it. That's the best service you can provide.

So how can an online entrepreneur provide great customer service?

> The first thing you have to get right is your product sourcing. If you get that and the quality of the product right you won't have any service problems.

And then you have to make sure your descriptions and information pages are easy to read and understand, so that people can understand what the product does; when there's no information missing, customers don't have to ask questions.

We do about two thousand transactions a week at the moment so that's about one hundred thousand transactions a year; but because our FAQ is so comprehensive, most customer questions are dealt with via the FAQ, which means we only need a person and a half in our customer service section to deal with any queries. It's a very cost-efficient way of doing business.

The shipping news: 'for free or not for free'

One of the first online success stories I heard about in the early 2000s was an American company that sold billiard tables online. I couldn't quite get my head around it at the time. Billiard tables? Those massive slabs of wood and marble, selling over the internet, sight unseen? How did they get them sent from one end of America to the other? How did people try them out? Didn't they want to touch them, feel them, see them before they buy? No, as it turned out.

This online billiard company turned over millions in its first year and now, of course, selling large, bulky goods — or as Paul Greenberg, founder of Deals Direct calls them, 'the uglies' — is commonplace. But the vexed issues facing all online retailers of 'the uglies' is the cost of shipping. Who should pay? The retailer or the buyer?

I recall the old days when buying a fridge or washing machine meant enlisting a distant cousin to lend you their trailer or having to source your own courier to come and deliver it for you. It was a big hassle, whichever option you chose. Now, of course, stores have their own delivery service, which makes it a lot easier. But one thing was — and is, for the most part, with traditional retailers anyway — still clear: the cost of delivery is at the purchaser's expense.

But what about online retailers? They seemed to have copped the raw end of the deal whereby they're expected to pay for delivery — even for the big 'uglies', which are hugely expensive to freight. Ever got a quote to courier a washing machine from Melbourne to Alice Springs? No, you don't want to know.

But that's exactly what John Winning, founder of the uber-successful online appliance retailer Appliances Online, has to grapple with each and every day. And judging by the 300 000 customers he has, he's doing a pretty good job of transporting those 'uglies' around the country. And he pays for delivery. Here's his rationale.

John: We didn't want to have these added fees and be a company that looks to be super cheap and then as they go and buy it they say, 'Oh, by the way you've got to pay for this and this and this and this'. And then, by the time you have added it all up it just confuses you with what you are paying for and you end up paying around the same cost anyway. It is also a legacy of my family's business that Winning Appliances has always had free delivery.

Bernadette: But doesn't that, like, cost you?

John: Yes, of course. There is no magic secret to how it works. It literally is wearing the cost and it does eat into your profit margin for sure, but it depends on what is engrained in your business DNA. We were used to absorbing that cost, we were willing to do it again and we thought it was going to be a competitive advantage in that hopefully we would make it up when we scale. So we just do it. We could charge for delivery and we would probably make more money, but it is not what we are about.

Our mission is to provide the best shopping experience in the world and we believe that free delivery is a significant part of that, even if it does cost us quite a bit of money.

The rationale is quite clear too that the benefits of offering free shipping will create significant word of mouth, so much so that the cost of shipping is offset by the extra business the favourable word of mouth creates.

> We could charge for delivery and we would probably make more money, but it is not what we are about.
>
> John Winning

Bernadette: Are there any other benefits?

John: We also save a lot of money through advertising because we get more people recommending us to family and friends so we get more word-of-mouth advertising rather than having to spend on TV and radio.

Shaun O'Brien of Selby Acoustics wasn't as keen to offer free shipping on his audio accessory parts but realised pretty quickly that not offering it made a big difference to the bottom line.

Shaun: We were starting to see our sales suffer a little bit because of the free shipping that our competitors offered. So we had to kind of go with it because all of our industry was doing it.

Bernadette: So, should everyone offer free shipping, no matter what?

Shaun: If you are in an industry that's not doing it, I recommend not doing it. It is a nightmare and yes, our sales went up but not as much as it would take to cover our shipping costs, so our overall profitability went down quite a lot and we are gradually trying to get that back.

But we genuinely went with free shipping. We didn't mark everything up to cover the shipping cost—we actually absorbed it, and totally did not change a single price point of our product. For small products we can get a flat rate nationwide, and free shipping works pretty well for something that cost $7 to deliver, but when you have to pay $177 to deliver—and that's a pretty reasonable example of what I've got with some of our products—it makes it very difficult to manage your budget and your profitability when you don't know what your costs are going to be.

As an online retailer, the choice is simple. You either pay for shipping yourself and hope the increase in sales volume covers the extra cost, or the consumer pays it and you hope like crazy a competitor offering free shipping doesn't enter the market.

Return to sender

Have you ever tried to take back a pair of shoes that don't fit? I feel nervous just thinking about an occasion when I had to do that, and it was one of those odd occasions when I hadn't even worn the shoes! The sales assistant turns them over and over in his hands, inspecting them more closely than a detective would a fingerprint. He looks up at me, weighing up my guilt, silently assessing my truthfulness. 'Have you worn them?' he enquires with a tone that suggests I have. 'Well, while I tried them on...in your shop...when I bought them...that was the only time,' I stammer nervously.

'Mmm, they look a bit worn here,' he muses, to nobody in particular, fingering the sole with his white, bony teenage finger. I feel under siege, as if I'm on trial. 'I swear, Your Honour, I haven't worn them!

> Our clients can return the shoes to us within 365 days as long as the shoes aren't worn.
> Jodie Fox

Ya gotta believe me!' After my trial is over, bestowing me with his good grace and mercy, he magnanimously offers me a credit note to be redeemed within an oh-so-generous seven days. Ah, service with a smile.

Jodie Fox, creator of custom-made shoes and owner of hard-to-fit feet herself knows exactly what it's like to return shoes, so she's made it a point to 'surprise and delight' her customers with what has to be one of the most generous returns policies on the planet.

> Our clients can return the shoes to us within 365 days as long as the shoes aren't worn. You can send them back to us and we will either remake them and ship the shoes to you straight away so that you can have them as quickly as possible, or we refund the full purchase price.

An unfortunate reality facing most online retailers is the cost of returns. Unlike retail stores, where the customer has to schlep their way back to the store to get their refund, online shoppers simply slip the unwanted item in a prepaid post pack, provided by the online seller, pop it in the post and get their money back, or a replacement product. As a consumer, I know which method I'd choose to get my money back. The anonymity of the internet has made returning goods a doddle. This is both a boon and a bugger for online sellers. On the one hand, it reduces the risk of purchase, so the consumer is more likely to buy something if they can return it with no penalty. On the other hand, consumers are less careful and more cavalier with their choices if they know they can return them, eroding the already diminishing margins that being online offers.

Sylvia, a 25-year-old media university student is quite breezy about the way she shops online.

> I always order at least three of the same garment. The size I think I'll be and one size either side of it, just in case. I just return the ones that don't fit.

That's okay for Sylvia, who gets what she wants with zero inconvenience and it's somewhat good for the retailer because they make a sale. But at what cost to the retailer? Not only do they have to have the stock on hand, they have to pick and pack it, pay for shipping out to Sylvia and then they have to pay for the cost of the return due to Sylvia's casual approach to selecting size.

But picking up the cost of returns is a way of life for any online retailer keen to be in business.

Shaun O'Brien has a very different approach to returns altogether. In fact, he doesn't believe in having a Returns Policy page at all. That's not to say he doesn't believe in the need for a returns policy. He just believes that a Returns Policy page sends the wrong signals to the customer.

Bernadette: So what do you call that page?

Shaun: We don't call it anything.

Bernadette: So what do you have?

Shaun: Nothing. We just don't have that page.

I feel like I'm in a scene from The Matrix. Who's on first?

Shaun: Lots of people use terms and conditions on their website. We don't. If you have 10 terms and conditions, that gives your customers 10 reasons not to buy from you. When I first shopped online, everybody would have a list of rules of what people had to do before they could buy: lots of hoops to jump through. It didn't make sense to me. I saw selling online differently; it's still a retail service industry, but because the person isn't in front of you and you're communicating by email, it's a lot harder.

> If you have 10 terms and conditions, that gives your customers 10 reasons not to buy from you.
>
> Shaun O'Brien

What I did though was anticipate likely problems my customers would face and build my customer-service system around what those likely problems would be. If you know what the problems are going to be, you have systems in place that avoid them occurring in the first instance. Being on eBay was great for that. We got lots of feedback about what worked and didn't. That really helped us refine what we do. It stands us in good stead. The ability to provide good service when something goes wrong, I think, is very, very important, but it's more important to avoid the problem in the first place.

Shaun has a novel tip.

> I suggest you get rid of the entire Conditions page altogether. If your website contains the right information about the product, the price, the delivery and the offer, then there shouldn't be a need to have any Returns Policy page.

Tim Davies, seller and education manager at eBay, has some good advice for online retailers wanting to create a returns policy that works, both for the seller and the buyer.

> For people wanting to start an online business, I think that helping customers feel comfortable buying from you online is really important, and having warmly-worded policies goes a long way in helping to create that feeling. eBay has spent years and invested heavily in ensuring that both the sellers and the buyers are protected

when buying online and we've spent years writing and refining our returns policy. My advice for online sellers looking for ready-to-use policies is to go to eBay's Returns page and see how we do it. It will save them a lot of time and energy instead of them having to create their own terms and conditions.

Money-back guarantee

This is a no-brainer. If you sell anything online (or offline for that matter), you must offer a 100 per cent, money-back guarantee. Don't worry, only a fraction of people will take it up (unless you've got a dreadful product) and the number of people who actually *buy* because of the money-back guarantee will more than make up for those lousy, stinking no-hopers who do come trudging back looking for a refund.

Like awards and testimonials, a money-back guarantee won't make people buy something they don't want, but it will help them overcome those last-minute jitters whenever they press the 'Buy' button.

* * *

Trust is without doubt the most important ingredient in any online success story. As you have seen, the entrepreneurs I interviewed invested heavily in creating it so that their customers would feel comfortable buying from them online.

If you don't have any customers yet, focus on how you can 'borrow' credibility by using industry association logos or attaching your product to other reputable organisations until you do get some customers.

Trust is an accumulation of a dozen or more different elements, such as winning awards, showcasing testimonials, providing photos of the products, offering contact details and being fast to respond, making sure your website has detailed FAQs that answer all the questions people are asking, providing free shipping (if you can), making refunds easy to process and offering an iron-clad money-back guarantee.

In isolation, each may not seem like much, but combined, they accrue to become a powerful testament to you being considered a trusted authority – the ultimate aim for any online business.

What's next?

In chapter 6 we look at the profile of businesses. I will show you how to create an online identity that's consistent with how you want to be seen in the marketplace and in that all-important court of public opinion, Google. Managing your online reputation and your personal and professional brand has never been more important. Chapter 6 shows you how to do it.

CHAPTER SIX
PROFILE

> I think (I am on Google), therefore I exist.
>
> *Bernadette Schwerdt*
> *(with a nod to Descartes)*

The Ricardo Montalban School of Entrepreneurship

Do you remember the classic TV show *Fantasy Island*, starring Ricardo Montalban as Mr Roarke, and his sidekick Tattoo?

In an interview explaining the trajectory of an actor's career, Ricardo famously joked about the five stages of an actor's career. He was kidding, but like all good jokes, there's an element of truth to it too. You can apply these same principles to the career of an entrepreneur:

- Who is Ricardo Montalban?

- Get me Ricardo Montalban.

- Get me a Ricardo Montalban type.

- Get me a young Ricardo Montalban.

- Who is Ricardo Montalban?

Whether you're an actor, a business identity, a sports star or a start-up entrepreneur, the lesson remains clear. Without active engagement and dedicated action, remaining relevant to your market can be tough. You've got to work at it.

Profile equals profit

When Deborah Hutton, the former model and TV host, launched her lifestyle website, Balance (www.balancebydeborahhutton.com .au), her motivation for doing so was to 'take control over my future' and to 'jump into the driving seat' rather than 'sit on the sidelines as a passenger'. She is reinventing herself as an online entrepreneur because she knows that, by her own admission, as she ages, the roles for her in the mainstream media dry up. She knows that profile is the name of the game and she's getting out there promoting her online endeavour in the media, just as we all must. She's got a head start: she's already famous. If you're not, how are you going to become a web celeb?

'I just want to do my thing!'

For the shy, unassuming or pragmatic entrepreneur, the thought of having to market themselves or build a public profile is anathema. Speak at an industry conference? Talk to journalists? Appear on a talk show? 'What a load of nonsense!' they say. 'I'll just get on with doing what I'm doing and let those other preening pussies have their time in the sun'. That is, until there's something they desperately want such as investors, government funding, an award or a senior business identity on their board. Then the benefits of profile kick in. But by then, it's too late. You just can't hurry profile. You can give it a nudge but, like building an architectural masterpiece, it takes time – unless you go with Metricon, in which case, it'll be up within a month. But I digress.

Most hard-working business owners just 'want to do their thing', whatever that 'thing' is – designing houses, painting portraits, building bridges, making clothes, singing songs, coaching kids or cooking cakes – without all the hoopla that goes into building a profile.

Well, I hate to break it to you folks, but we all need to market ourselves, no matter who we are or what we do. Even organisations such as meditation centres, yoga schools, kindergartens, hospitals and cancer charities, need a profile to survive. If you think about it, online entrepreneurs need a profile even *more* than most because they often don't have a store or a tangible product to show or promote, and the majority of their work is done behind a computer. No, it's not fair, or right, or fun. It just is.

Harry M. Miller sincerely believed that the media was there to do the client's bidding, not the other way around. 'Use the media before they use you,' was his mantra.

Those who hustle get the highest profile and those with the highest profile win.

Stephanie Alexander is under no illusions as to the power of profile, especially when it comes to promoting books.

> In this day and age, sadly, I think profile is very, very important for marketing. Publishers have taken a big hit from the digital industry so they have less money to spend and they are not particularly interested in splashing the sort of money on marketing that they might have done 10 years ago. So if you have got your own profile you attract a market and they like you.

As an author, she knows that profile equals profit.

> If you have a profile that is able to command an audience, you're a boon to a publisher. If you can speak to a group of people that really want to hear what you have got to say then you're doing half the publisher's job for them. But it's good for you too. I used to do lunchtime speaking events with *The Cook's Companion*. They could just come, pay their $20, have a nice lunch and go away, but they were fabulous for generating sales. If you don't have that sort of profile it removes a very effective tool for the publisher.

> In this day and age, sadly, I think profile is very, very important for marketing.
> **Stephanie Alexander**

Stephanie Alexander and Deborah Hutton are experienced media professionals and already have high profiles, yet they are still actively engaged in building their brands. If you want to become a web celeb, you need to take action to make it happen. The media won't come calling; you have to generate your own attention.

The journey to relevance

You might be thinking, 'Hey, I'm just an employee. It's not even *my* company, and I never want to write a book anyway, so I don't need to worry about building my brand'. But what if you leave, get sacked or are retrenched? What then? You'll be in the market for a job, competing with others just like you, and that's when profile really does count. Maybe you're not in the newspapers or the social pages, but what about your social media profiles? Are they up to date? Have you been 'working the room', building your industry connections, speaking at business conferences and getting known by those who matter?

I interviewed Peter Williams, Chief Edge Officer at Deloitte's Centre for the Edge and asked him how important it was for senior managers to be highly connected on social media; that is, to have a profile. He replied:

> It's essential. If I'm recommending someone for a job, a board position or a role of any sort, one of the first things we do is check their social media pages to see how active they are. If they're not connected, tweeting, blogging or contributing to the industry conversation in some way, it's a sign to me they're not in touch; that they're not staying relevant with what's happening.

> If I'm recommending someone for a job, a board position or a role of any sort, one of the first things we do is check their social media pages to see how active they are.
>
> **Peter Williams**

As online entrepreneurs, we too are always looking for 'work', be it in the form of new clients, joint ventures, investors, media attention or awards.

The message is clear. Irrespective of what position, business or industry we're in, profile is the name of the game. You should be building your brand no matter who you are, what position you're in or what you do.

What's a personal brand?

If you ask people to name the entrepreneurs they most admire, three people tend to get nominated. We all know who they are: Richard Branson, Steve Jobs and Oprah Winfrey, the poster boys and girl of entrepreneurial success.

It's no surprise. All are visionaries and have achieved incredible success.

But what is it about these entrepreneurs that has captured the imagination? What is it about them that appeals to others?

Yes, they have high visibility. Yes, they are charismatic. Yes, they are hugely successful.

What they also have in common is they have all constructed their entire organisations around their personal brands.

Their identity is at the core of all their enterprises. They are the sun around which all their planets (businesses) satellite, shining heat and light wherever they go.

(I find it interesting that we rarely, if ever, see/saw the people *behind* Richard, Steve or Oprah: the thousands of senior managers who run their companies and make operational decisions. It was always Steve on stage, Oprah on the couch, Richard on the dais. By accident or design? Make no mistake, these entrepreneurs are the stars of their own shows.)

If you look closely, you'll notice they've done very successfully what most entrepreneurs want to do, and that is, they've built successful personal brands, product brands and company brands, with themselves at the centre of each. Brilliant! Figures 6.1, 6.2 and 6.3 (overleaf) show, in visual form, what I mean.

Figure 6.1: Richard Branson is at the centre of his empire, irrespective of what product or division he is promoting

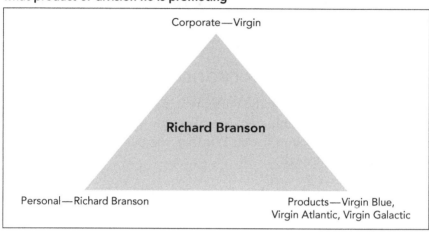

Oprah has done the same.

Figure 6.2: Oprah's personal brand is intimately woven throughout all her products and companies

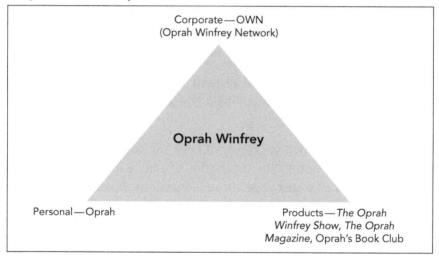

Apple has also done the same. Will the brand be diminished in Steve Jobs' passing?

Figure 6.3: Steve Jobs was at the centre of all things Apple

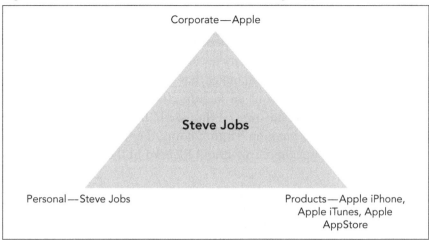

Have a think about what your 'branding triangle' will be (see figure 6.4).

Figure 6.4: Consider putting your personal brand at the centre of all your business activities so that they all benefit from your increased profile

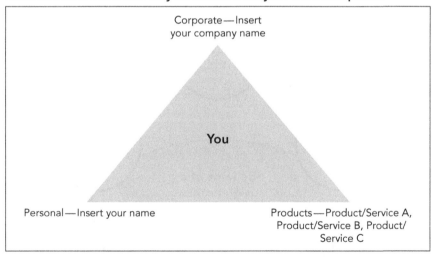

Put yourself in the centre of the circle, 'the sun' so to speak, and then insert the products, services or divisions that will each benefit from you increasing your public profile.

The genius of this strategy is that when you promote yourself (as Richard and Oprah do), all your products and services get promoted at the same time.

Caveat emptor:

The danger of this strategy is that when one person represents the entire brand, as Steve did, and that key person dies (or leaves the business), it can destabilise the entire company because the 'hub' from which all the branding for the company emanated has disappeared. This leaves the brand rudderless and without an identity. Imagine if Richard Branson passed away or left the business? Who would become the 'face' of the business? It's hard to imagine Virgin getting the same level of PR and goodwill it currently generates without Richard in the picture.

The Profile Expansion Cycle (PEC)

There are major benefits to having a high profile. Take a look at how the Profile Expansion Cycle (PEC) works to get a clear understanding of why profile equals profit (see figure 6.5).

Figure 6.5: There are major financial benefits to having a high profile

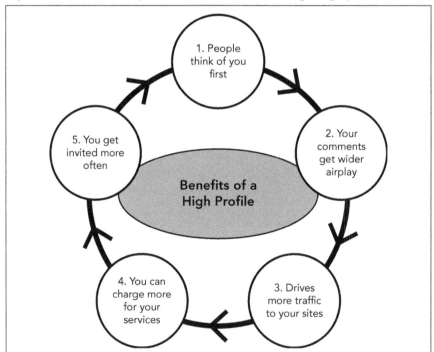

Note: By the way, this PEC is a TLA (three-letter acronym). All great entrepreneurs know that coming up with a TLA to describe a process or a system is the fastest way to develop thought leadership. Having a TLA makes you sound clever, even if you're not! (It may even land you a speaking gig or a book deal!)

Why you must have a high profile

When you have a high profile...

1. *people think of you first.* This means you get invited more often to:

   - speak at conferences

   - sit on boards and panels

   - write guest blogs

   - appear in the media

   - comment on industry matters.

   All this is good because...

2. *your comments get wider airplay.* This means that:

   - more people get to hear about you

   - more people trust you.

   All this is good because...

(continued)

Why you must have a high profile (cont'd)

3. *it drives more traffic to your sites.* This means that:

- you increase the numbers on your database and social channels

- you get more leads and sales.

All this is good because. . .

4. *you can charge more for your services.* This means that:

- you can spend time working on the business, not in the business

- you can spend more time on profile-building activities

All this is good because…

5. *people think of you first.* This means that you get invited more often to:

- speak at conferences

- sit on boards and panels

- write guest blogs…

…and the cycle continues.

Creating a personal profile may seem like yet another thing you have to do in order to build a successful online business and I can't help but agree. For those of us who just want to 'do our thing', putting into place these profile-raising activities can be exhausting. But you only have to look at the entrepreneurs who've done exceptionally well to see that behind all those carefully crafted media stories there's a very sophisticated and well-oiled PR machine in operation.

> **Tip**
>
> Come up with a TLA (three-letter acronym) for a process or system you've developed as soon as possible. It makes you sound smart.

The rise and rise of the personal brand

The concept of personal branding — where *we* are the brand — didn't exist 20 years ago. Sure, products and services had brands, celebrities had brands, and even politicians did (a bit). But business owners? It was unheard of, except if they were a major identity such as Kerry Packer or Alan Bond.

Now, entire sections of book stores are devoted to biographies, autobiographies and misery memoirs from people we've never heard of, simply because they have an intriguing story to tell.

They won an Oscar. They ran a marathon. They got shot. They robbed a bank. They got kidnapped. They lost a leg. They sold a lot of makeup.

Why are they writing books? Because they like writing? No. Because they're egotistical, fame-seeking hounds trying to keep the burning embers of their notoriety alight? Not that either.

Why? Because they *are* the brand and they know that if their personal profile is high, their business profile (and income) will benefit.

Why do you think Carman's muesli founder Carolyn Creswell is one of Australia's most sought-after public speakers? Because she likes it? Possibly, although with four young children I bet she'd rather be at home reading bedtime stories.

I don't know Carolyn personally, but I would suggest she has carved out a successful public-speaking career because she knows there's a bunch of me-too muesli manufacturers hot on her heels, edging their way into that sweet little 'yummy but healthy' niche she's had tied up nicely for so long. She's under threat, like all of us, and she's doing something about it by getting out there and building her profile. She's talking to as many people as she can, giving samples to everyone along the way, and leaving a trail of good feelings wherever she goes, in the hope that it will rub off when the grocery buyer of the household pans along that enormous aisle of brekky cereals, looking for a reason to choose a box of muesli among a sea of copycats.

The rest, as they say, is history

We all love a good story, but journalists love them more because a good story sells more newspapers.

That's why they're always looking for the angle, a 'way in' for the reader to connect with the story.

Think of any well-known 'girl/boy makes good' story and there'll be an angle to it that gets played out in the media over and over until it becomes folklore. For example:

- JK Rowling, a single mum struggling to feed her child, writes stories in cafés to keep warm, writes a best-selling novel...and the rest is history.

- Russell Brand, an out-of-control, drug-addicted wild child on the verge of a drug-induced breakdown, gets discovered at a comedy night...and the rest is history.

- Nicole Kidman, a mildly successful, flame-haired Australian actress gets discovered by Tom Cruise, appears in his next movie...and the rest is history.

People love stories! Especially when the person completes the Hero's Journey and overcomes great obstacles, finds a mentor, has success, falls back down, nearly gives up, tries again and succeeds! The story line is as old as *Jaws*, and all those other Spielberg movies.

The one-liner test: what's yours?

Location: radio station
Producer: We need an outspoken, Sydney-based mummy blogger to talk about how the paid maternity leave scheme will benefit mothers. Who can we get?

Location: office
Sales manager: We need a female speaker on gender imbalance in the workplace who's had experience working in a predominantly male sector. Who can we get?

Location: the pub

Conference planner: We need a big, boofy sports star who loves a beer and can talk about the glory days of cricket in the 1970s. Who can we get?

I know it works like this because I've been present at all three scenarios, and the conversations run pretty much just as I've described.

Can you see what's happening? People's needs get condensed into one-line descriptions:

- 'Sydney-based mummy blogger'

- 'female speaker who's worked in a predominantly male sector'

- 'big, boofy sports star who loves a beer' (mmm, spoilt for choice there).

If you had to write your own one-liner to describe you and your offering, what would it say?

When you know what that is, you can promote it and get the word out.

Here's a story of a previously unknown entrepreneur who knew exactly what her one-liner was and caused a media sensation that saw her booked on practically every TV talk show across the country.

Neryl Joyce is a single mum who left her job as a check-out chick at Woolworths to become a soldier in the Australian army. Following this she went to Baghdad as a protective services officer to guard senior figures in the military, a private bodyguard of sorts. When she came back from Iraq, she wrote a book about her experience, *Mercenary Mum*, and spruiked it on the TV shows. Here's the angle that virtually every show ran with:

- Babies, bullets and Baghdad: meet Australia's *Mercenary Mum*!

- *Mercenary Mum* becomes a Baghdad bodyguard!

- From checkout chick to *Mercenary Mum*!

The motto of the story: be clear, and certain, about the angle you promote, because if the media like it, you'll be stuck with it! Fortunately, it worked for Neryl.

What's your one-liner, your elevator pitch? In other words, what's your story?

What's your story?

Marketers often talk about 'value proposition'. This is just a fancy phrase for 'What do you offer?' or 'What do you do?' It's also known as your 'elevator pitch'.

Some people think that phrase is out of date but I don't. Far from it.

In a sound-bite world, we need to be able to pitch our idea quickly and succinctly, and twist it to suit the person we're talking to. We humans are a self-interested lot so we tend to only listen to another's pitch if we feel there's something in it for us. That's why you need to come up with a pitch that solves a problem for the person you're talking to. The best way to do that is to come up with a unique solution that only you can offer. It's called your unique selling proposition (USP).

Finding out your point of difference or unique selling proposition is equally important. Here's a simple fill-in-the-blanks template that will help you discover your USP. This process also helps you put it into a simple sentence that describes what you do, why you do it and how it helps others.

Fill-in-the-blanks USP template

Who am I?

'I love _____ but was fed up with _____. So I created _____ that_____.'

Here are some examples of the template in action (name the company, if you can).

Who am I?

'I love beautiful shoes but was fed up with wearing shoes that looked awful and didn't fit right because the stores never stock my size. So I created an online shoe design service that lets women design their own shoe so they look beautiful and fit perfectly.'

Answer: Shoes of Prey

Who am I?

'I love drinking wine but was fed up with friends paying too much for wine that wasn't worth it. So I created an online wine service that helps people buy the wine they want, at great prices, educates them about what they're drinking and delivers it to their door.'

Answer: Vinomofo

Who am I?

'I love building online businesses, but was fed up with the cost of using expensive web-development agencies. So I created a platform that enables business owners to connect with individual web developers from around the world to cut out the middleman and reduce the costs.

Answer: Freelancer

By using this template, you are not only defining who you are, you are also giving your customers the phrase to use when telling someone about you.

Try it yourself

Here's the USP template broken down into components.

Here are some handy rules to follow when you fill in your USP template:

- Keep it to two sentences.

- Describe what you have done, rather than what you will do.

- Keep your product names out of the sentences.

- Don't over-think or over-complicate.

- Solve a problem for people.

- Keep it simple and clear.

- Write it for one person, not a group.

Here's my perception of the USPs created by some of the entrepreneurs I interviewed. Most of them aren't reinventing the wheel, but just offering an existing service with a twist (see table 6.1).

Table 6.1: some great unique selling points

Business	USP
Temple & Webster	Beautiful items for the home, beautifully priced
Catch of the Day	Daily deals on a wide range of products at amazing discounts
Milan Direct	High-quality designer furniture at great prices
Vinomofo	Great wines, curated for you and delivered to your door
Shoes of Prey	Design your own shoes online to get the perfect look and fit
Appliances Online	Brand-name appliances at great prices, offering extreme customer service with free delivery
Who Gives a Crap	Environmentally-friendly toilet paper that helps fund sanitation projects in developing countries
Thankyou	Bottled water (and food and body-care products) company that donates profits to developing countries and enables the buyer to track what project their money went to
Cook's Companion app	Vast array of easy-to-find recipes, logically stored in one place that's cost-effective and easy to use
Freelancer	Comprehensive range of creative services at discounted prices
Booktopia.com	Buy Australian, support the local economy, and pay a flat-rate shipping fee no matter how many books you buy

What's *your* personal brand?

Have you ever thought about what your own funeral would be like? I have. I think about: Who would come? Who would give the eulogy? Who'd be the hard-core supporters who'd go to the burial and stay for the cake and coffee in the church hall, and who'd be the blighters who nick off at the first opportunity? ('Sorry for your loss. Gotta dash!')

I fantasise about the nice things people will say, the photos they'll show of me, the stories they'll tell of what a kind and compassionate woman I was. I picture the mourners touching the coffin gingerly as they pass by on the way back from communion. Sometimes I cry just thinking about how emotional my funeral will be for me. But I digress.

Let's pull the lens back a bit and assume that your funeral hasn't happened yet; that you're in good health and that life is dandy.

But I *do* want you to imagine what you'd *like* people to say about you when you're gone. But wait, let's pull back even further. If I were to do a random, anonymous survey of 10 of your closest clients, suppliers, colleagues and friends, what would they say about you *today*?

To create your pitch, or elevator statement, or 'story', you have to work out what people think of you *now* and then work out what you want them to think of you in the future.

Here's a personal branding audit to help you with that.

Take the Personal Branding Audit (the PBA—another TLA!)

I have developed a cheap and easy 'branding audit' process that helps you quickly identify what your stakeholders feel about you now.

It's best done in a team environment but beware, you may hear things you don't want to hear. Only the bravest sign up for this exercise, but it's very illuminating and, as they say, it pays to 'know thyself'.

The personal branding audit

This is how I conduct the personal branding audit in my client workshops. You can adapt it for your own purposes.

Step 1

I put up on the screen a series of well-known logos (Apple, Virgin, Qantas, and so on) and I ask the audience to shout out the very first thought, feeling or impression that comes into their head when they see it.

Step 2

I write down the words that come up as I show the logos. For example, I'll show the logo for:

Apple

Here's what people generally say about it:

- visionary

- clean

- fun

- expensive

- Steve Jobs.

When I put up the logo for:

Virgin

Here's what people generally say about it:

- irreverent

- Richard Branson

- fun

- inspirational

- value for money.

When I put up the logo for:

Qantas

Here's what people generally say about it:

- safe

- reputable

- Australian

- reliable

- that annoying little Irish guy.

Step 3

I then put up on the screen a series of well-known faces and ask the audience to shout out their feelings, impressions or thoughts. Here are some of the responses I get.

- *Angelina Jolie:* gorgeous, humanitarian, refugee advocate, Brad, mother-of-six

- *Quentin Bryce:* classy, smart, kind, well-dressed, diplomatic

- *Clive Palmer:* the audience just laughs!

- *Gina Reinhart:* censored due to legal reasons.

Step 4

And then I put up this picture:

The room goes silent. You can hear them thinking:

'Wow! What would the group say about *me*?'

The mirth and laugher from a moment ago dissipates. Why? Perhaps for the first time in their entire careers they've really had to wonder, 'How do other people see me?' Maybe it's because they have never thought of themselves as brands. 'I'm just me!' they say. But aren't we all brands?

Make no mistake. This is a fun and funny exercise, but it's very confronting and it has real and deep consequences for those who do it. It's one of the few times we ever get to consciously think about the exact words others would say about us.

What participants in this exercise discover is that how they are currently perceived by others is not how they want to be perceived. In other words, there's a gap that needs to be bridged.

I then ask them to think about what kind of behaviours, activities and qualities they would need to exhibit if they wanted to be seen in a particular way.

Know your persona before you start

As an entrepreneur, knowing how you're currently perceived is integral to knowing how you *want* to be perceived. Here's how I discovered what total strangers thought about me.

I attended a weekend stand-up comedy workshop in Melbourne a number of years ago. It was run by Judy Carter, a brash, fast-talking American comedian.

One of the first exercises she had us do was tell a three-minute story on stage in front of all our classmates. As we performed, the audience was given an index card and asked to write down exactly what they thought of the performer in a no-holds-barred way; they could write whatever they liked.

When it was my turn, I got up and told a story about the small role I played in the TV show *Blue Heelers*, where I played the mum of a young boy who had been mauled to death by a tiger in suburban Mt Thomas (those pesky tigers, you just never know what they're going to do next!). I talked about the show and how disappointed I was that after my episode aired the entire show, one of Australia's longest running shows, got cancelled, which I took quite personally.

The comments written about me ranged from mildly positive ('looks like an air hostess'; 'reminds me of my mum/Toni Collette/Liza Minelli') to the downright offensive ('could lose a few pounds'; 'needs her roots done'; 'don't like her shoes'). Confronting, but strangely helpful.

Why did Judy put us through that? Because she believed that in order to be a good stand-up comic, you need to know what persona you emanate before you even set foot on stage.

Your persona – the way the audience feels about you before you've even opened your mouth – is integral to the type of content you can deliver. If you're a gorgeous, skinny, tanned supermodel getting up complaining about how tough it is to land a date, sorry, you're gonna be blasted off the stage. 'Tell someone who cares!' is what the audience will think.

Imagine if Chris Rock got up on stage and told jokes about his maid, his driver, his luxury lifestyle? His audience would boo him off! His schtick is 'black kid from the wrong side of town makes good' and drawing attention to his wealth and affluence would detract from his persona.

It's the same for an online entrepreneur building their personal brand. If you were born with a silver spoon in your mouth, and everyone knows it, it would be wise not to be putting forth the 'I started in a one-bedroom apartment living off 2-minute noodles' story. People won't buy it. In fact, they'll punish you for it and your brand will suffer: 'What would he know!' they'll think. 'I could do what he did if I was born with money!'

You have to know 'your persona' before you start building your personal brand. The public won't mind which way you go, but just be honest with your story.

How to build a profile

As you can see, to be a successful entrepreneur you need to invest in building a personal brand. This helps promote you, but of course the end result is that it promotes your business.

There are a couple of practical steps you need to take to build a personal brand. They're not difficult, but they do require a bit of courage, persistence and dedication.

But think about how many years you plan to be in business, and know that putting in the work now will almost certainly pay dividends in the long run.

Buy your personal URL domain name

The very first thing you must do is realise that no matter who you work for or what you do, *you* are the brand so you must go out, right now – yes, now – and buy the URL for your own personal name, aka vanity domain, not to be confused with a vanity URL, or a vanity basin. But I digress.

In the not-too-distant future, our personal websites may be the first port of call for people wanting to contact us. Check out www.crazydomain.com.au or www.godaddy.com now and see if your first and last name are still available and buy it. It's not expensive (less than $20) so do it now and do it for your children too. They'll thank you for it later.

> *Tip*
> Buy your personal URL domain name today!

Google yourself first

Thought leaders around the world live in fear of one thing: Google! They know that their credibility lives and dies on what Google says about them. These days, it's not who we say we are, it's who *Google* says we are.

Control over the conversation about our personal and corporate brands has gone and we need to get it back! But how? By creating compelling, persuasive content that lands precisely where you choose, at the right time, in front of the right people. That's how.

When was the last time you googled yourself? No, it's not pretty, is it? And that's why most people don't do it. But in the interests of self-awareness and knowing where to begin your online identity audit, it's worth doing.

Mastering this process is the art of content marketing. If there was ever a time to learn the strategic process of how to manage your personal and professional brand, it's now. In a world where reputations, sales and profitability rely on minimising risk and maximising trust, learning how to manage your online identity is an essential tool.

Build a website for your personal brand

Now that you've got your message clear, your USP sorted out and your branding on target, let's look at the tools available to help you spread the word to the world about how fantastic you are.

If you want to build a personal brand to support your business profile, you'll need to create your own personal website. This should be in addition to your business website. Whatever you want – whether it be a personal or business website – Mark Middo has some great advice on how you can get one up quickly and cost effectively.

Bernadette: So what's a good way to get a website up, Mark?

Mark: I have a framework I use called 'The 3 Cs' and I find it an incredibly helpful tool when coaching entrepreneurs. It's straightforward, easy to remember and it works.

Bernadette: What do the 3 Cs represent?

Mark: They represent the three most important components of any online business:
Castle, Content, Communication.

The Castle is the website. To succeed online you need to have a good website in place first and have the right branding that looks like it cost you $50000 but really costs you less than $200. It's really important to have an awesome-looking site straight away so that you can match it with some of the other competitors straight away. Impressions are everything.

The next C is for Content. Obviously the content area is important. You have to create content that people are going to like; that resonates with them.

The next C is for Communication. It's about getting that content out into the marketplace: getting yourself out there, getting some media, getting some PR and 'lighting spotfires' on the web.

Bernadette: What does 'lighting spotfires' mean?

Mark: It means getting on forums, on blogs, commenting on others' blogs, 'Liking' pages, retweeting tweets: getting yourself out there to really promote the castle that you have created and the content you have written.

Depending on what you sell, you could consider setting up a business website to sell your products and services, as well as a personal site to promote your own brand.

There are loads of ways to set up a website. All of them will take you longer than you think and cost more than you thought but there are some shortcuts you can take.

Bernadette: What website platform do you use?

I love WordPress because you can't just see it as a website, it's an online marketing platform. You've got full flexibility, you can add plug-ins, and increase the amount of people in your database very quickly.

Bernadette: But finding what you want your site to look like is one of the most time-consuming factors. Any hints on how to get something up fast?

Mark: Jump onto www.themeforest.com and go looking for some WordPress templates or themes. The best way is to look for something in your niche and start from there. For example, if you are a personal trainer, search for a 'personal trainer theme' and you can see a full array of sites that relate to personal training. It will give you a way to compare one site to another and work out what you like and what you don't. You can grab yourself a theme for a fraction of what it would cost a web developer to build.

Tony Nash is a big believer that to look like you mean business, you need to look the business.

> If you're a $20 million business, you should aim to look like a $100 million business. And that's what your website needs to do. It takes longer than you think.

Jodie Fox has a neat trick to share.

> There is a gap between the way people communicate with developers that causes a lot of problems. A website like MockingBird (www.gomockingbird.com) is great as it helps you to mock up all of the pages you want on your website that you are going to share with your developer. It's a really good way to communicate with the person who is going to put a website together for you.

She's also an advocate of 'start small and just get it moving'.

> You don't need to have a perfect thing first off the bat. You need something that works. You need to work out that people actually care about the concept you have put together before you put a whole bunch of money behind that one thing. I set up a website for myself recently for my professional speaking work and I think it cost me $100 to buy a template for that and it took me a couple of hours to put everything up and make it look streamlined. It's not rocket science.

What about if you need a customised site. Will WordPress do?

Mark Middo's advice is:

> Don't invest in a customised website until you're really sure you have a going concern. So it's best to stick with WordPress first before you invest big bucks in a full-blown site.

Kate Morris has some advice that only an experienced online marketer can know.

> Having been through my fair share of disastrous web projects, the advice I'd give is to make sure there is always a penalty clause if things go over time or things are not delivered as per the scopes.

Stephanie Alexander also had some challenges setting up her app:

> We considered four different developer groups and they all had totally different ways of presenting what they thought the cost would be. So it was quite difficult, and if you're like me and don't know anything much about establishing a digital product, it's very,

very hard to look at those figures and say, 'well that's the same as that quote'.

My advice would be to draw up a contract where you say 'I am not prepared to vary this more than 10 per cent' or something like that, but it certainly varied a lot from the original quote to what we eventually had to pay.

Create great content

If you google yourself and you have your social media sites up and running and well-populated, you can be certain that the first results that show up will be your own social media pages.

This is important because when clients or the media search for information about you, you want to make sure they see the content that you want them to see. Without these pages available, Google will find random mentions of you and list them first. This is your chance to control the conversation.

> **Tip**
>
> Get up to speed with search engine optimisation (SEO) to get your site ranked. This is a non-negotiable skill and will set you apart from the competitors.

Take a long-term view with your content marketing. Google has a long memory so take the time to get the content and the strategy right, and ensure that the only content that leaves your desk is something you'd be happy to see in a year, or five years' time. Proof it, let it sit for 24 hours (at least) and then send it. Measure twice, cut once!

Content marketing is the new black, so it's worth taking the time to find out how you can manage your online identity. Googling yourself is a start — if you dare!

Here's three ways you can use content to build your online identity.

1. Give your content away for free

The first principle you must get comfortable with is giving away content for free. James Tuckerman of Anthill Online has this to say about the freemium model.

> We grew up in a different world where the modus operandi was 'the margin is in the mystery': where we don't tell anyone how we do something so that we can go and do it for them and get paid a fee.
>
> There's a lot of people still operating under this obsolete view. Every mystery is now available in a five-minute YouTube clip, so nothing is a secret anymore.

He's not referring to IP or trade secrets, but to your expertise, the process or technology you have developed that makes you good at what you do.

> **Tip**
>
> Be okay with giving away things for free.

Why are celebrity chefs so rich? Is it because they give away all their recipes on TV, at the supermarket and online, or is it because they know that people are inherently lazy and that we'll take the easy option and buy the recipe book with everything in it, rather than try and bookmark a dozen recipes on random sites?

Darren Rowse knows aggregation works too.

> We have loads of blogs in our archives, but sometimes people can't be bothered searching back to find what they want so when they see we've put the 'greatest hits' in an eBook, they are more than happy to pay for it.

2. Create high-quality content quickly

Getting as much high-quality content as you can out into the marketplace is an essential tool for getting on page one of Google, and also for demonstrating your thought leadership on your topic.

Personally, I like to record webinars, and then get them transcribed so that I can then slice and dice the content and create blogs, FAQs, tweets, posts and fact sheets out of the master content that I've created.

Sometimes I speak directly into my voice memo app, get that transcribed and my speeches or blogs are practically written for me. It's very time effective and often I like to write as I speak so this makes it even quicker to write content.

3. Use a creative brief to kick-start the copywriting process

Having worked as a copywriter for more than 20 years, I know lots of shortcuts to writing copy that will literally carve hours off your writing time and give you a better result.

In Appendix 2 you'll find the Creative Briefing sheet I use whenever I meet a client. I ask my client each of the questions on the sheet in order and before too long, I have all the 'raw material' I need to get me off and running.

I could write a manual on how to write copy (hang on, I already have!), but this will at least give you the basic questions you need to ask before you start writing any copy.

You may not have all the answers to each question, but if you can't answer a question, just make a best guess and move on. We can never be sure our answers are right, so we just have to get on with it

Copywriting is a delicate combination of art and science and if there's one skill you should really become good at that will make a difference to your bottom line, copywriting is it.

There are loads of ways to create content that can position you as a thought leader.

Mediums for promoting yourself

There's a range of mediums to get your word out to the world, but here are the most popular ones:

- YouTube: the largest video broadcasting website on the internet

- Facebook: the world's largest online social network, where you can feature your profile and your business page

- Twitter: a microblogging site and a great way to share and receive up-to-date news with a worldwide audience

- SlideShare: share your IP here by uploading your PowerPoint or Keynote presentations

- LinkedIn: the biggest online directory of professionals; make sure you have a company page set up too

- WordPress: a cost-effective way to create a blog.

Become a skilled public speaker

Once you've got your site up and running and you've got some great content on the site and on Google, you'll need to start drawing attention to yourself. There are all sorts of ways and we cover many of those in the next chapter (Promotion), but one of the greatest ways to increase your profile and leverage your thought leadership is to become a compelling public speaker. Here are four ways being a good speaker can be great for business.

1. It helps you grow your database

When I wanted to drive traffic to my new www.copyschool.com site back in 2006, I contacted networking organisations that featured lunchtime speakers. I got on the speaking roster, attending lunches in Sydney, Melbourne, Adelaide and Brisbane (at my own cost), and at the end of the session made a compelling free offer to the attendees in exchange for their email contacts. And voila! Within a month, I had nearly 1000 names on my database.

2. It increases sales

Having a big database means you get more sales, leads and enquiries. It's a numbers game, and when you have a big database, your email newsletters become your de-facto sales force. Instead of ringing clients to 'see how they are', sending a relevant, timely and engaging email can convert prospects into sales better than a 'how are you going?' phone call ever could.

3. It builds credibility and fast-tracks prospects into clients

Why meet with one client at a time and scrabble to establish credibility when you can speak to 100 people at a time and have your credibility established before you've even taken the microphone? If you're any good, you'll have people lining up at the end of the event waiting to do business with you.

4. Stage an event yourself

Why wait for an event manager to choose you as a speaker? Why not stage the event yourself? My student copywriters often face this early-stage dilemma of how to build a client base. One of my students, Nick, was retrenched from his senior role at a major computer company in Melbourne. With a wife and two young daughters to feed, he had to get moving quickly to generate income as his retrenchment package was on the low side due to the short time he'd been with the company.

I said, 'Do you know a printer?' Yep. 'A business coach?' Yes. 'A graphic designer?' Yep. 'A web developer?' Sure. (As a newly minted member of his local networking group, he knew lots of other people with similar target markets to his.) Great! Host a networking evening, get them all to present for 15 minutes on their topic, get them all to send the flyer to their databases, share the costs and, bingo, you've just increased your database by at least 100 people in one fell swoop and positioned yourself as an expert.

He did all that. The event sold out. He built his database exponentially and he established his credibility with ease so that the clients approach him now, rather than the other way around.

Become known for a process

One of the hardest things for entrepreneurs offering services is to turn their service into a product that's scalable. Services can be hard to sell and they're often connected by the umbilical to the expert (you), which means unless you're delivering it, you're not making money. As we've already established, the old 'trading hours for money' model is not a great model for online entrepreneurs.

Sam Chandler, co-founder and CEO of Nitro (www.gonitro.com), knew that selling email and web services was always going to be limited by how much time he could put in.

So he created a document alternative to Adobe Acrobat that enables users to annotate the actual document, knowing that a scalable product was going to be a lot easier to sell than time-for-money services.

This former high school-entrepreneur-from-Tasmania-turned-Silicon-Valley-darling raised $US15 million in funding from American investors and his plan is to take it public in the future. In 2014, he told the *Sydney Morning Herald*, 'What I learnt from that experience is that service companies are really hard – they are hard to scale and to manage,' he said.

But turning your intellectual content into a process is a guaranteed way of scaling your online business, not to mention getting more speaker bookings, getting known for your expertise and selling successful information products.

Service providers often succeed online by creating membership sites and they're great for business owners who love to keep footloose and fancy free and travel the world. You can deliver a webinar, a coaching session or a Skype call from anywhere in the world and you can scale up without incurring extra costs.

For example, servicing 100000 people every month rather than 100 people doesn't necessarily involve 100 times the effort, but the income ramps up significantly. One hundred people paying $35 per month is $3500. Imagine 100000 people paying $35 per month? That's $3500000 per *month*. US-based corporate coach Michael Hyatt is allegedly doing just that. The numbers are phenomenal.

Fast on the coat tails of Michael Hyatt is James Tuckerman, the creator of Anthill Online. He's built a membership site with more than 20000 subscribers and he can make serious money by running a webinar or simply recommending another person's product. He's taken time to build his list and his subscribers know he delivers quality content. They trust him, which is why they're happy to pay a small amount per month for access to his content. They know it's going to be good.

Five million readers follow Darren Rowse's blog every week. Even if Darren sold a $100 product to just 1 per cent of them, he would get $5000000. I'm not suggesting he does, but imagine if he did. Nice work if you can get it.

> **Tip**
> Become known for a process.

Don't let anyone tell you an online service business can't make money. There are lots of benefits to having a service-based online business too – you create the product (or control the quality of the ones you recommend) and you don't have to worry about delivery, cost of production, repairs, size issues or the fear the supplier may go out of business.

* * *

If you're an online entrepreneur and you really want to 'own your space' and be known as the best at what you do (your USP), you need to identify what that is and then go about creating an online identity that presents that story to the world.

Once you've done that, you need to consider whether you'll be the face of the brand. If you decide you will, then you need to create a personal-branding story that resonates with the public.

Before you do that, it's important to understand how you are currently perceived by your market and how you want to be perceived by your market.

When you get clear on your USP you need to create content that demonstrates that USP and amplifies your thought leadership.

Your overall objective is to ensure that when people Google your name or business, the only content that shows up is content that supports your brand identity.

The best way to do that and to push down any negative Google results is to provide Google with lots and lots of great content.

What's next?

Promotion is the art of driving traffic to your site, finding new customers and creating great content that's relevant, engaging, easy to read, gets found on Google and presents you in a way that enhances your personal brand.

And that's exactly what we'll cover in the next chapter.

CHAPTER SEVEN
PROMOTION

Better to remain silent and be thought a fool
than to speak out and remove all doubt.

Abraham Lincoln

One big mistake entrepreneurs often make is they start thinking about promotion too early in the marketing process. For example, they start thinking about how they're going to promote the business before they've even worked out what they're going to promote or who they're going to promote it to. It's putting the cart before the horse and it's a recipe for wasting money on promotions that don't have a hope of working.

That's why I've left this chapter until last.

As you can see, there's a bunch of thinking and strategising that needs to take place before you start building your website, or writing blogs or creating videos, but once you've done the thinking, everything will take a lot less time to create because you'll know what you want to say.

So let's assume your site is up, your branding is in place, you know what you sell and what you stand for, you're out there speaking and you're doing a good job of it all. Wouldn't it be great to have some other tools to get your message out there faster?

As you'd be aware, the methods for promoting an online business could easily fill 10 business books, so I'm going to focus on the mediums that the entrepreneurs I spoke to felt delivered the best bang for their buck. Most are working to a budget and few have millions to spare, so you can guarantee that what they've done has been measured to within an inch of its life, and that it works.

So let's start with what is the most vexatious issue for any online entrepreneur. This is without doubt the most asked question by small business owners, online entrepreneurs and bloggers at any forum I run: 'How can I drive traffic to my site?'

How can I drive traffic to my site?

If you have money and you don't mind giving it to Uncle Google via an AdWords campaign, then getting traffic is a no-brainer. But what if you have a brand-new site, with no customers, little content and a fledgling idea and you can't wait for traffic to come along? Mark Middo's got some good news for you. It's called growth hacking.

Mark: Growth hackers focus on low-cost and innovative alternatives like social media and viral marketing instead of buying advertising through more traditional media such as radio, newspaper and television. We focus on growth first, and budgets second. I use it to build a database quickly. For us, it's about getting traffic to a site quickly, building a database so that you generate revenue quickly and developing super-fast ways to make all that happen on a regular basis.

Bernadette: So how do you do it? We're all ears.

Mark: Firstly, try to make 'sharing' part of your user experience. One of the most famous growth hacks was done by Dropbox, the cloud-based file sharing system. They did not have a huge budget to work with to run a marketing campaign, so they needed to figure out a way in which they could leverage their current user base and also leverage the newest customers to grow their subscriber base.

Bernadette: What was their hack?

Mark: They made sharing part of the experience by getting people to share the Dropbox tool with their Gmail contacts and if you did, you got an extra two gigs of space straight away. It wasn't a cheesy contest where you see people saying, 'Share us on Facebook and you have a chance to win'. It was about getting people to really share something of value with their friends. You 'hack your growth' by thinking of things to get people to share. Facebook, Twitter and Airbnb have all used growth hacking really successfully. The vast majority of people who signed up to Dropbox started sharing the product with their friends, facilitating huge viral growth and turning them into one of the largest online businesses in the world. Their user base exploded to four million within 15 months, a 3900 per cent increase. Sixty per cent of these new sign-ups were from the referrals.

The 4 steps to becoming a growth hacker

Here are Mark Middo's top tips on growth-hacking techniques that can be used to build your database quickly and cost effectively.

1. Take the time to understand your target market's online behaviour and identify the large networks they use on a regular basis. Is it Facebook or Twitter? If you are a restaurant, is it Yelp or Urbanspoon?

2. Make sure you have a referral program set up for new users where you incentivise them for sharing your product or service with their friends—just like Dropbox did.

3. Test, tweak and repeat. Once you set up this system, add analytics so you can see the results, then start to put new users through it.

4. Keep improving until you can look back at it and say, 'I know that 50 per cent of my customers who purchase my product will tell their friends about it through this system'.

You may recall that Simon Griffiths built 'shareability' into his crowdfunding video with incredible results.

> People just wanted to tell other people about what we were doing and they started posting photos of our product on social media, which led to our sales just increasing, increasing, increasing and now we've got a very successful online business selling toilet paper. It was all about making it shareable.

Growth hacking is not for everyone. Darren Rowse has taken his time to build up his database and he has good reasons for doing that.

> Getting people quickly is the hard part. I have never really done that. You can get a lot of readers quickly, but they are quite often the wrong type of readers and that could do more damage than good by getting snappy comments. I have certainly had that happen to my blog.

> I don't just want readers. I want the right readers.
>
> **Darren Rowse**

> The key is to really think through who you want to reach and so that is part of a mindset shift. You really want to think through, 'I don't just want readers. I want the right readers'. So I always say to people identify who you are trying to reach and then work out where they are hanging out online or offline and then go and be useful in those places.

Matt Barrie knows a thing or two about getting traffic to a site.

> There are a lot of ways to get traffic to your site. It really depends on the business you're actually in. The major internet companies in the world have all basically done it through harnessing what I call 'distribution fire hoses' on the internet: the big sites like Facebook. In simple terms, you've got to really figure out effectively how to get referrals. You need to get your customers happy enough to share the experience with their friends and then with their friends and so on. And that's how you get the viral loop going.

Pay Per Click was a great source of traffic for Temple & Webster, says Brian Shanahan.

Brian: We started off with just doing Google AdWords like most online businesses and we spent a lot of time around optimising our landing pages, optimising our copy on Google, doing lots of A/B testing.

We found that the keywords 'beautiful items for your home' delivered much better results than 'get up to 70 per cent off homewares'. We see the results of our online marketing initiatives within minutes, which allows us to continually iterate around testing, learning and optimising. This ability to iterate so rapidly is one of the great things about online marketing.

Bernadette: How much money should a business spend per day, when starting out?

Brian: We started off with just $100 a day and I think you would be very surprised about the depth of insights you can get with that spend. Then, when you find a keyword that gets the right returns, you invest your money in that keyword and expand your tests to similar keywords.

Bernadette: Is there a law of diminishing returns with Pay Per Click?

Brian: Yes. You can get to a point of diminishing returns where further spend on a keyword results in lower returns. For example, when you're ranking #1 in search results, investing more in that keyword won't get your ranking any higher. When we got to that point of diminishing returns with paid search, we started to invest in other channels like Facebook, offline, print, TV and Out Of Home. We've found that Facebook and print are particularly good marketing channels for us – principally because these formats are more visual than paid search – and one of our strengths is our beautifully styled product imagery.

Bernadette: What's the value of testing?

Brian: It's really important to do lots of testing and analysis. Learnings are key to making every dollar go further, regardless of whether your budget is a few hundred dollars, or it is a multimillion-dollar campaign.

Here's how ProBlogger Darren Rowse gets traffic to his blog.

Any time we publish a new blog post it gets alerted on our Twitter account automatically. And within 24 hours of publishing something, we have written about it on our Facebook page. We also offer to alert people via email whenever we publish a new post. And then we also do an end-of-week newsletter which summarises all the new posts for the week.

As a blogger you want to give people a variety of different reasons to subscribe or follow, depending upon the way they use the web and who your audience is. For example, I have quite a few retirees in Digital Photography School and they don't want to receive emails, as they don't understand RSS feeds and they are not on Twitter. But we need to really understand who we are trying to reach and how they use the web.

But according to Darren, when we focus on fast growth, we overlook one of the most basic tenets of good business.

Darren: Look after the readers you have already got. You may only have 10 of them, but they are all important and the more impact you have on them, the more you respond to their comments, the quicker the word will spread.

I used to email every new reader I had on my blog. If anyone had left a comment I would send them a personal email thanking them for commenting. So going over the top for those readers is really important.

Bernadette: How else we can build traffic organically?

Darren: I recommend you get off your blog and start interacting on other people's blogs, participate in their forums, write guest posts on their blogs, engage on social media or anything like that. Being in other people's faces is really important.

Bernadette: What's the difference between a blog and a newsletter?

Darren: A blog is typically a bit more personal in style and an ongoing conversation on an array of topics. You can be a bit playful with it. However, generally what makes a blog a blog is that the articles are ordered chronologically rather than just by category; they usually have comments, and are dated.

How can I monetise social media?

Social media is being used in all sorts of ways to promote business.

Here's how Simon Griffiths used social media to launch his crowdfunding campaign. Critically, he built the concept of being 'shareable' into the campaign from the outset.

Social media for us has been our number-one marketing tool. It's how we drove traffic from the crowdfunding campaign where it's all about that shareable, viral content. And I think a really clear example of that is the fact that *The Age* and the *Herald Sun,* the biggest papers in Australia, didn't cover us until the third day of our crowdfunding campaign. It was 48 hours before the newspapers came out with a story on it. We generated almost all our sales from social media. By the time the newspapers had come out with the story, we had almost reached our target. So for us it's all about social media.

> We generated almost all our sales from social media.
>
> **Simon Griffiths**

Now that we've got the product out there, we're getting people to take photos of what they're doing and placing that on their Twitter and their Facebook, getting them to talk to their friends on Facebook and telling them about who we are, and that's what drives all the traffic to our site.

Global copywriter Belinda Weaver, from Copywrite Matters, promoted her business via Twitter and was impressed with the results.

I started sending out tips and hints on how to write copy to my growing Twitter base and after a while, the referrals just started coming in. The tips helped demonstrate my thought leadership and it also showed that I understood how to use Twitter, which drew in more too. I made sure each tweet led back to my site and this proved to be a really cost-effective way of sourcing new clients.

James Tuckerman, founder of Anthill Online is adamant that there's only one real way to make money from social media.

> If you want to monetise social media you have to get your customers and prospects off social media! Get them onto your website, get them into your database, get them into your meeting rooms, get them into your coffee shop, get them into your workshop rooms, get them into your demo days, but get them off social media!

Not everybody is delighted with the onslaught of social media and Stephanie Alexander's comments probably resonate with more than just a few.

Stephanie: I am pretty jaded about social media. I do have a presence on Instagram, I do have a really nice website, I do have a business Facebook page and I get a good response from people, but I can honestly say it hasn't at this point influenced sales. So it just leads me to wonder why you do it.

I feel a little more fond of Facebook and certainly I have my own email newsletter, which I really love doing. This goes to faithful people who have been alerted because of the Facebook page, so they wouldn't be subscribers to my newsletters if I hadn't had the Facebook page. So I have to acknowledge that fully. But I do feel that when I put a lovely picture on Instagram, I would like to have a response from the public that's something more than just 'yum'.

> I would like to have a response from the public that's something more than just 'yum'.
>
> Stephanie Alexander

Bernadette: What would be an ideal response?

I suppose I'd like to know if somebody actually made it!

Jodie Fox has some simple but insightful tips on how to get the most from social media.

> Engagement is probably the most critical metric that we look for. Interestingly, I started signing off my posts with my name and I think

once people realised that there was a real person there to talk to it became much more personal for them, and they were more willing to engage.

She was very clear also on what social media's true purpose is: 'It is a community-building exercise and not a sales exercise'.

But the final comment rests with Simon Griffiths: 'The golden rule for making something shareable is that you just have to take your pants off!'

> Engagement is probably the most critical metric that we look for.
>
> Jodie Fox

How can I use PR to create media attention?

A large number of online entrepreneurs I interviewed engaged PR agents, and the stories you see in the media about them are generally a result of their activities. But some entrepreneurs, especially when starting out, preferred to manage the media themselves.

Jodie Fox was one of them.

Jodie: We outsourced our PR in the US market for a couple of years but the reason that I prefer to do this in-house now is because you have perfect control. You also have that person just thinking about it and completely invested in your company.

Bernadette: Any tips on how to get good PR?

Jodie: It's often about having the patience to find the right journalist. It's being thoughtful about which story you share with which journalist so you don't waste their time. You want to help them to do their job so you have to make sure you know their style and the topics and the angle they are going to be interested in. Journalists get a lot of pitches so you are going to be doing a lot of following up as well. Getting face to face with journalists is really important.

Andre Eikmeier does it differently.

> We outsource our PR but we work with them every day and meet with them every week and receive regular reports from them. You've got to treat it like they are part of the business.

Stephanie Alexander has had regular exposure in the media for decades, which may explain her position on PR.

> I don't have a PR agency and I could count on three fingers probably the number of times that I had dealings with PR agencies.

> I've got a bit of a cynical view about PR, and I feel the same about advertising. You can't discount it, but it's practically impossible to get a real handle on what it is achieving for you. I would never be comfortable spending large amounts of money on it.

Brian Shanahan from Temple & Webster says:

> PR is important but it really depends upon what you are trying to achieve and where you are in your growth lifecycle. Some companies invest in PR too soon—there's no point investing in PR if you haven't got a great product to promote!

Of course, getting coverage is one thing. Making sure you get the coverage you want is another matter. When a journalist comes calling, you'd better be prepared. After all, not all PR is good PR.

Here are some tips from journalist and media trainer Theresa Miller on how to make sure you make the most of your time in the sun.

Theresa: The media can make or break your reputation overnight. Before you commit to an interview, ask the journalist a few questions, such as, 'What angle are you taking?'; 'Who else are you interviewing?'; 'When and where will this story be published/broadcast/tweeted/posted?'

Bernadette: *What if they come calling and we're not ready for them. Any tips on how to manage a 'door-stop' interview?*

Theresa: Firstly, don't comment if you aren't prepared. Instead, smile sincerely and offer any of the following comments and then zip it. 'I'd love to help you, but I don't have that information right now' or

'I don't have time now.' 'Why don't you give me your details and we'll set up an interview later today when I have the time and that information?' That will give you time to work out your key messages and strategy.

Bernadette: How can we keep control of the interview?

Theresa: Before any interview, work out two or three bullet-proof key messages you'd like to get across no matter what you're asked. This will help you take control and give you something to fall back on if you're stumped by a question. These are short, sharp and always positive. Some examples might be:

- 'Our company is committed to staging fun, entertaining family-friendly events.'

- 'All our equipment complies with Australian safety standards and we take that very seriously.'

- 'Our price increase is in line with inflation and still represents great value for money.'

- 'Our online vocational courses are run by top-rate tutors who are industry leaders.'

Bernadette: How long should our 'grabs' go for?

Theresa: 'Grabs' or 'sound bites' for TV and radio are around six to eight seconds. If you don't want to be edited and taken out of context be sure your quotes are short, punchy and powerful.

Does TV still work?

When you're killing it online but you can see your growth plateauing, do you as an online retailer say:

a) Well, that's the end of growth for us

b) We should spend more on Pay Per Click

c) We should advertise on TV

For John Winning, that was the scenario he faced.

> We're an online pure-play retailer and we had significant market share so rather than trying to wait for the market to naturally penetrate from offline to online we thought it is really our job to fuel that growth. So our strategy has been to get more people to shop online. We can't get the growth numbers we've been used to by just waiting for customers to come to us, so we are at that point where we need to just drive those customers to the internet.

The TV networks will be happy to hear John's perspective.

> A large number of people watch TV and as far as we're concerned, TV's not dead until people are not watching it anymore. Online advertising is becoming more and more expensive and we find that the cost of an eyeball is probably not that dissimilar from what it is on radio or TV. So in terms of value for the money spent it is probably very, very comparable.

TV has been great for Temple & Webster too, says Brian Shanahan.

Brian: We wanted to work with The Living Room TV show as they have a similar demographic to our target customers, they have an engaged and growing audience, and they're a fun and creative team.

When we have a feature on The Living Room on Friday nights, I grab a glass of wine, and am on my laptop as the show goes to air.

We monitor the number of visitors we have coming to our site, the number of member registrations we get, site speed and what products they are attracted to. There is typically a huge surge in activity immediately after Temple & Webster is mentioned.

Bernadette: Were you surprised at the result?

Brian: Yes, I was surprised! The initiative was so successful that the amount of traffic we received actually crashed our site for a few minutes, so we learnt a little bit more about how to scale our web infrastructure that first night, but people have clearly got two or even three screens in front of them, and it is amazing how quickly people come to the site and start to transact during and after the show. That's one thing I love about online: you can see instantly the impact your campaigns are making – there's no waiting until next week – it's today and it's now.

The power of email marketing

I received an email recently that had the subject line, 'Your copy sucks'. It shocked me. Who could say such a thing to me, a copywriter? What were they looking at? And more importantly, how did they know? My brain went into overdrive dealing with the emotional and psychological trauma of being found out to be what all writers think they already are: a fraud.

And then I realised. Duh. It was spam.

Huge sigh of relief. All is okay with the world. Faith in myself has been restored. My copy doesn't suck. (Does it?)

So who said everyone ignores email marketing? That one subject header got to me, and of course, that's the point. You've got to 'get' to people, but in a good way.

Here are a couple of sneaky email subject headlines I've received lately. They're spammy, and slightly creepy, and I don't necessarily recommend using them, but they got through to me:

- Bad news
- I'm sorry
- I was thinking about you
- Can we meet up?

If you want to create ethical headlines that actually represent what you do and are on-brand, the biggest tip I can offer is to be one of two things, or both if you can. And they are:

- be useful
- be entertaining.

Jodie Fox knows the power of regular communication with her prospects and she works hard to make her emails useful to her clients.

Here are a couple of email subject headlines she has used. Chances are she got the headlines from a question or a comment in a blog from her clients, a brilliant way to source email newsletter content.

- 3 ways to make the best of black

- How to wear metallic

- New! A heel shape you'll love

- What shoes to wear with jeans

- 5 shoes to have in your wardrobe

- How to find your ideal heel height

- Sale! 20% off black shoes for Black Friday

Andre Eikmeier considers emails to be an important reflection of his brand, Vinomofo.

> We made the choice that if we are going to be bothering people, we are going to try and be entertaining and a bit witty, get rid of the jargon and make it fun, and that worked for us.

> When we write our emails, we write as if we were speaking to a friend or a relative standing directly in front of us, and that shapes and influences what we say because you wouldn't try to sell something that you didn't believe in to a friend. And we have trained our whole team to be that way.

Email campaigns: tips and tricks to getting great results

Email marketing is one of the most cost-effective strategies for driving conversions and sales, but the downside is that you need a good-sized database to make email marketing work for you.

But if growth hacking a database is not your style, here's some other tips on how to build a big database quickly.

How can I build my email database?

As you'd expect, Mark Middo has a solution for building databases.

> To build an email list really fast you have to create a squeeze page which has only one specific action and that is to get them to give you their email address. To get that email, you have to give away something for free like a little eBook or some sort of guide that's really targeted to whoever you are targeting. So let's use the example of the Japanese technique to remove cellulite.

> You might say, 'Here are 10 tips the Japanese know that are secrets to get rid of cellulite' and then you give away a little 10-page guide to it and it's just a basic introduction to that product. You can then start to build a targeted list of people from it and then you can sell your product later on. Facebook is probably the best way to really get targeted traffic.

Shaun O'Brien has a few tips.

> You can buy a list, but that's a waste of money, because it is not followed by traffic. If you've got your site up and running and you want to start building a mailing list in particular, you've got to give something away, like a monthly draw or a competition. Every time we do something like that we build our list by another thousand in a month, but you've got to be consistent.

> Big promotions work too. Every now and then we offer 15 per cent off and we do around twenty-two times the normal base sales.

> We don't do them very often, which is why they work—they are credible and we are not just shoving products down people's throat.

Temple & Webster also uses the 15 per cent discount offer. I wondered if there was something magical about the number 15?

Shaun O'Brien had done the testing.

> We've done 10 per cent before and we've done 20 per cent before. Twenty per cent worked really well, but it cost a lot to run that level of discount so we found that 15 gave us a good result without taking

too much off the bottom line. And we've done 10 per cent off once and that didn't make a massive difference, so 15 has been about right for us.

Jodie Fox adds:

We did a series last year where I shared a favourite outfit of mine for brunch, one for going out and one for poolside and I asked people to design a pair of shoes against each of those over a period of a couple of weeks and the winner won four pairs of shoes. That competition increased sales and that happens after every competition.

Temple & Webster has a brilliant method for generating email addresses. In order to log into the site, you have to give them your email address. Or you sign on with Facebook or Twitter.

Kate Morris of Adore Beauty has this to say about lists.

It's really important to remember that quality is better than quantity, and I'd sooner have 100 customers on my list who are going to buy something than 100 000 who aren't.

You need to remember your ABCs: Always Be Collecting. So every single touch point, every single activity that you ever do, make sure there is a signup — offer email signups everywhere. If you have got a front counter in your store, have an email signup there. If you go out and do events, make sure that you've got an email signup wherever you are potentially reaching new customers.

> I'd sooner have 100 customers on my list who are going to buy something than 100 000 who aren't.
>
> **Kate Morris**

Jane Huxley, managing director of Pandora Internet Radio, says that when they collect data they always focus on PAG: postcode, address (email) and gender. In the United States, where their head office is based, their data-collection process is so sophisticated, and they have so many people on file, that they can actually predict how their customers will vote in a political election!

How important is search engine optimisation (SEO)?

On the topic of getting a website on page one of Google, all the entrepreneurs were in agreement: you've got to know how search engine optimisation (SEO) works.

Matt Barrie had this to say.

> On a normal day, two billion people spend most of the time punching little words into Google and getting blue links spat back at them. If you can figure out a way to use Google effectively through either search engine optimisation or search engine marketing then that can be very effective for some businesses.

I wondered if Darren Rowse of ProBlogger worries about SEO when he writes his blogs.

Darren: I don't ever let SEO dominate my writing process. I much prefer to write for human beings than a machine. However, when polishing up an article, it is useful to ask the question, 'How would people search Google for this term?' and imagine what terms people are using. And then you might want to use those keywords or phrases in the title of your post, or in your headings, naming each file with those keywords, but I don't tend to get into deep analysis on that front. I am interested in writing the best content, but it doesn't hurt to know some basics about on-page search engine optimisation.

Bernadette: YouTube is the second most popular search engine. What role, if any, did video play in your success?

Darren: I have used videos on ProBlogger and it certainly drew in a different type of audience. Some people are much more visual. They like to hear things rather than read things. When I started doing videos I was just using talking-head videos and I found that some readers tended to really react differently to that and I started getting comments from people I'd never heard from before. So that helped. It is worth doing.

Bernadette: And can it help with SEO ranking?

Darren: I think that is where it is going. They are certainly ranking videos as well as other types of content and I expect that will continue, with search results including video content. A lot of people transcribe the videos and then put the transcription on their blogs so that their ranking is not based on the video but on the text as well.

Here are Darren's top tips on being a blogger:

- Be useful.

- Understand your reader.

- Meet their needs as much as you can.

- Be regular.

There are other kinds of blogging too. One of these is guest blogging.

How does guest blogging work?

Darren Rowse also knows a little bit about guest blogging. According to Darren, guest blogging is one of the fastest, cheapest and easiest ways to get your blog on page one of Google and noticed by the thought leaders in your industry.

Bernadette: What is guest blogging?

Darren: Guest blogging is when you leverage someone else's blog to get at their audience. It sounds a bit selfish to 'use' someone else's blog for your own purposes so it really needs to be a win–win interaction.

Bernadette: How does it work?

Darren: So I have a blog. It has been around for a while. People come to me and say, 'I would like to write a post on your blog. I will do it for free'. And in return they get a link back to their own blog where people can learn about them.

Bernadette: Is it a bit like being the warm-up act at a concert?

Darren: Yes. You don't go to see the warm-up act. You go to see the main act, but while you are there you see these other great acts and you want to check them out. It's about building your online presence through their blog.

Bernadette: So how do you get to be a guest blogger?

Darren: It's about building relationships with other bloggers, pitching topics to them that relate to the audience that has not been covered on their blog already. It's wise to start with some smaller blogs and then work your way up to bigger blogs as you develop your profile. You want to really put your best content on these other blogs as well.

Bernadette: But what if you're little Johnny Nobody from Lower Butt Creek with no authority or credentials? What do you do then?

Darren: If you can't guest blog, write a thoughtful commentary on a thought-leader's blog and put it in their comments section. Chances are it will be read by the blog owner and by their readers, so it's a neat little way of getting your content read by a thought leader who would not otherwise have heard of you.

Here's the lesson from that. Other sites may have a higher 'authority' than your own, so getting featured on those sites can have a very positive effect in raising your profile on Google.

The benefits of guest blogging

If you have a new site and it's not being ranked on page one for your preferred search terms, you're going to have to wait a while and produce an awful lot of optimised content to get on there. So why not take a shortcut and just guest blog as much as you can for others: industry association websites, industry journals, networking associations and so on. The benefits will be three fold.

Firstly, they'll welcome the content because they probably don't have enough content for their blog anyway. Secondly, you'll look really generous and helpful by offering to write the blog. And thirdly, your blog is likely to be read by your colleagues and clients, positioning you as a thought leader in your industry.

Blogging with a purpose

According to Sandy McDonald, author of the book *Get It Right Online*, blogging has the potential to do more than drive traffic to a site. She believes it can also help you build a community of passionate advocates.

A successful business blog is one based on the intersection of purpose and research. When a business owner aligns their purpose, communications and customers to a common cause for mutual benefit and to uplift lives, they have the ingredients from which to create a fiercely loyal and advocating clan.

Done well it's a paradigm shift because it changes a business conversation from 'what can we sell them' to 'how to make a difference in their lives'. And yes, there's a commercial benefit to this.

Today, our customers are our marketers and if we can create a clan of passionate followers who believe in us and what we are trying to achieve, they will become our greatest source of new business.

So how can you start blogging with purpose?

> It's very simple. Every time you have a conversation offline with someone who poses a problem that you know your business can solve, write a post about it. You can send that person a link to that post to demonstrate how you've solved their problem.

This is a considerable investment in time and effort, but according to Sandy, 'the rewards of building a community who love what you do and will shout it from the rooftops far outstrips the investment'.

'Community' in business terms can mean just a few people who advocate across the online space for what you do, or it can mean thousands of people all actively working together to achieve an agreed outcome.

Blogging is key to building both and it's fast becoming the 'new' way to build an online community.

How to build an online community

Creating a community is one of the fastest ways to build awareness, because the people in the community become your biggest advocates and fans.

Most people love being part of a community because, in today's online world, it's easy to feel isolated and disconnected from other people. Wanting to feel part of a 'tribe' is perfectly natural. These days our tribes are often focused around our interests. It's not just for social reasons; our community is also where we learn, find mentors and grow.

Valerie Khoo has been very successful in creating a community for her business, the Australian Writers' Centre.

Valerie: People would meet and connect through our courses. We'd have informal meet-ups and the community grew from there. But we realised that if you want to foster and grow a good community, you need leaders, structure and a strategy for its future.

So we made sure we invited people into our community and gave them resources and activities that were exclusive only to our members. That way, we really added value to our 'tribe'.

Bernadette: How did you build the community?

Valerie: First, we connect via social media – it's easy, free, and it's a great way for our community members to connect with each other, too. We also invite students to join certain Facebook groups that focus on specific genres of writing, so there are even 'mini-tribes' within our larger community.

Bernadette: But doesn't it take a lot of time to manage a community?

Valerie: When you have an engaged community, they often self-organise. So then it's just our job to monitor what's going on and support what they are doing. That's the power of the community. You don't have to do all the heavy lifting because everyone in the community is so supportive.

Bernadette: So what are the commercial benefits of facilitating a community?

Valerie: When our students have a good experience, they tell their friends. So when they are part of a dynamic and valuable community, they become great advocates for us. It's wonderful to have such avid fans because they encourage their own friends and social circle to discover our courses. It's like marketing on steroids!

---

5 steps for building a community

Here are Valerie Khoo's top five tips on how to build a community.

1. *Communicate regularly.* This could be with something as simple as a weekly or fortnightly newsletter.

2. *Offer exclusive resources or services.* Provide resources or services that are tailor-made for your community and ensure that they are offered to them exclusively.

3. *Leverage social media.* Determine one or two social-media platforms that your community members are most likely to use. Establish a presence and start connecting.

4. *Provide encouragement.* Lift members up. Congratulate members when they have kicked goals. Share this with the rest of the community.

5. *Demonstrate leadership.* Understand that you're a leader. People like to know what is expected of them and appreciate it when there are clear guidelines and rules for how the community will operate.

You are leading this tribe. You need to provide advice on your chosen field, and a structure so community members know what to expect. Be consistent so people know what to expect and when.

How to connect with teenagers and digital natives

One of the most difficult communities to get in touch with are those at the forefront of the digital revolution: the digital natives.

If you have a product or service targeted at teens or digital natives, you have to do things differently. Traditional channels just won't cut it. So I asked my good friends Sonya Karras and Sacha Kaluri, co-founders of the Australian Teenage Expo and two of Australia's leading speakers on cyber bullying and safe partying to provide some tips and hints on how to connect with this demographic. They speak to literally tens of thousands of school children every year, so they know what works and what doesn't.

I asked Sonya and Sacha for their top tips for marketing and connecting with young people.

Sonya and Sacha: Social media is the key to marketing to young people and it's all free, so make sure you have at the very least a

Facebook page, a YouTube channel, Twitter, an Instagram account and even a hashtag (#) you want people to use.

Social media is the key to marketing to young people.

Sonya and Sacha

Bernadette: How can we interact with them when we're on social media? Any tips on getting through?

Sonya and Sacha: Competitions on social media always work well. It might be getting them to come up with an idea as to how they can put together a clip to promote you. U2 asked young people to post a clip of themselves singing their latest single and to put it online, with the winners getting tickets to their concert. Imagine the traffic it created.

Bernadette: What about the copy? Long or short?

Sonya and Sacha: Keep it short and succinct. Young people bore easily and will not stick around unless it grabs their attention immediately. Get to the point quickly.

Bernadette: We can't not talk about selfies. How can we bring that into the conversation?

Sonya and Sacha: This generation is brilliant at documenting their lives through photographs. Try to get them to take a picture of themselves with your product or logo in the picture. Your brand could go viral at the hands of that young person who has posted it on social media.

Communicating with digital natives is not complicated but it may require you to step outside your comfort zone and become more familiar with how social media operates. Even if you don't use it, they do, so that means you need to as well.

How to outsource effectively

About now, you're probably thinking, 'well this is all well and good, Bernadette, but I'm a busy person! I have a job to go to, a partner to satisfy, a bunch of kids to scold, a dog to shout at and three months of box-set DVDs to get through. How on earth am I going to get all these websites built, and how am I going to pay for all these blogs, videos and social-media pages? And who's going to do it all?'

Keep your hat on. That's what outsourcing is for.

What is outsourcing?

I first heard the word many years ago from a female corporate warrior friend of mine who was appointed as the CEO of a major listed US company at the age of 13 (that's not quite accurate, but she was a very high achiever at a young age). She said to me in a most emphatic way, 'Bernie, outsource everything as much as you can: cleaning, bookkeeping, the garden, the pool, child minding, cooking, washing, sex with the husband...' (No, she didn't really say that last bit.)

But I was shocked to hear that she felt it was okay to outsource all this stuff. Now, it's commonplace to outsource all that and I do...well, as much of it as I can. Except the bit about sex with the husband. But I digress.

> You could actually outsource everything if you wanted to. The critical thing is you keep whatever is core.
>
> Matt Barrie

Outsourcing all the grunt work for your business is now the secret to being super-efficient and it can really take the load off if you're just getting started and don't want to invest too much time or money.

You can't talk about outsourcing without talking to the king of it, Matt Barrie of Freelancer.

> You could actually outsource everything if you wanted to. The critical thing is you keep whatever is core—the core intellectual property, or the stuff that you love doing. You can keep that to yourself and do the things you do best.
>
> But all the things you don't want to do and all the things that are mundane or repetitive or 'grunt' work you can outsource. Here's a classic example. You might run a small business that sells through a website and you might hate dealing with answering questions from people every day and updating the website and sending out email newsletters.

You can hire a virtual assistant now for about three hundred dollars a month who will sit there, do all the customer responses, update your website, update your product descriptions, send out newsletters and so forth and you don't have to do that anymore. You can just focus on finding great products to sell or maybe some sort of creative marketing or whatever your interest is.

Mark Middo, author of *5 Minute Business*, agrees.

You can't be good at everything so it's better to get people who are specifically good at some things to do the things you can't. I've taught myself how to code, but only at a basic level, and there are lots of back-end things that I can't do. My time is better spent working on developing a business and writing copy rather than sitting there banging my head against the wall trying to figure out why a piece of code doesn't work.

But there's one task that most did not want to outsource, and that was social media.

Kate Morris of Adore Beauty feels quite strongly about it.

Personally, I don't really believe in outsourcing social media because it should be a direct reflection of your brand and a direct reflection of what you are doing internally. And as a key customer-service channel, it's not appropriate for us to outsource.

Simon Griffiths isn't a big advocate of outsourcing at all.

If we're talking about coding something on our website then we probably need to pay a coder to do it if we can't figure out how to do it ourselves. But nearly everything is done in-house, from customer service through to the building of our online store through to a lot of graphic design. Eventually, as we grow and get bigger, we can put systems in place and then move away from doing it all ourselves. And it means that we now know how every single part of the business works and we build systems that allow us to build ourselves out of the business so that we can then focus on the next thing.

Andre Eikmeier has firm thoughts about this too.

You can't just outsource a key part of the business like building a website and hope it works. We outsource some SEO because the team that we outsource to is good at it, but it only works when we really put the time in. We outsource fulfilment and delivery stuff, but again, all the headaches come from when we don't pay attention to it. They all have to understand what you stand for and how that particular element of the business works in the bigger picture.

This chapter could have been a book in itself. There's a lot to promoting an online business, but I've focused here on the strategies that the entrepreneurs felt delivered most 'bang for their buck'.

They included techniques such as growth hacking, social media and PR to drive traffic to a site. We discovered that TV is not dead after all and that if you really want to become a world-class online entrepreneur, you absolutely need to understand search engine optimisation and be an outstanding content creator.

We looked at email marketing, and some great email offers that have been proven to work.

For those without large databases, Darren Rowse took us through the ins and outs of guest blogging, surely one of the most effective ways to build a database quickly at zero cost. He also let us in on a sneaky trick that will get our blogs in front of thought leaders even if we're a nobody!

Both Sandy McDonald and Valerie Khoo elaborated on the power of building a community and how an active group of advocates and raving fans can deliver tangible commercial benefits.

And for those targeting digital natives, it has become plainly obvious that the cheapest, fastest path to their hearts, heads and wallets is through social media. What a surprise!

Of course, one of the biggest obstacles to online success is finding the time to build the website, write the blogs, send the emails and shoot the videos, but we have a solution to that too. Outsourcing is fundamentally changing the way we do business and paving the way for those with a limited budget to really make their mark.

TAKE ACTION:

THE SEVEN-STEP ACTION PLAN TO CREATING A WILDLY SUCCESSFUL ONLINE BUSINESS

Successful entrepreneurs don't emerge from the womb already formed and ready to go. As you've seen, they, like most people, had to start from scratch and claw their way up, rung by rung, to get to where they are today.

So what's next for you on your journey to online entrepreneurship fabulous-ness?

Are you keen to take that hobby, passion or idea and turn it into an online business? I encourage you to say 'yes!', because if you don't, someone else will. In this dog-eat-dog world of online business, you've got to move fast. Ideas are a dime a dozen but it's the execution that counts, so do something about it now.

Maybe you're already online but just need a boost and some clarity on what you're doing and why and what needs to happen next.

7-step action plan

No matter where you are on the timeline of your online 'journey', this seven-step action plan mirrors what we covered in the book and will help you get going. While you review it, take a pen and start jotting down some of the ideas that come to mind. This will form the basis of your 'next step'. You don't have to do *everything* right now, but you do have to do *something*.

The top 50 free apps you need to know about

I've created a comprehensive list in appendix 1 of free business apps for you to review. Take a look at them before you begin this exercise as you'll discover that there's an app for some of the tasks, functions or activities you need to put in place to build your online business. There's no need to pay for services like file sharing, email marketing, webinar recording, website development and so on until you really need to, and these apps will provide you with the stepping stones to getting your business up and running without spending a cent.

Here's a summary of the seven-step process to help you get started.

Step 1: Purpose

Get clear on your 'why' – do you want to make extra money, or do you want to make it your life? Do you want to be a disrupter and dominate an industry, or do you just want to build a business that pays for the school fees and a family holiday each year? Maybe you've already got a flourishing business but want to amplify your online presence?

Action: Write down the top three reasons why you want an online business. What will it give you? And what will *that* give you? Why do you want that? Keep drilling down until you uncover the 'nut' of why you want an online business.

Step 2: People

You need to build a team around you that will support your vision, provide expertise you don't have and hold you accountable. There's a lot of elements to building an online business – branding, copywriting, graphic design, web design, web development, email marketing, social media – and you need to know a bit about them all. If you're struggling with any aspect of getting the business going, chances are it's because you have hit a roadblock related to one of these areas. Often we don't know what we don't know, which makes it hard to get things moving.

Action: Type into Google the exact question you would like to get answered, no matter how silly or basic it might seem. For example, how do I set up an auto-responder? How do I upload a video to YouTube? What comes up will give you some resources that will take you to the next level of understanding and then you can refine your questions accordingly. If you have a question, Google has the answer.

Step 3: Planning

You need to be confident in what you're selling, that it has a market; that the prototypes work; and that testing has been conducted.

Here's where the rubber meets the road. Start researching your idea using the tools mentioned in chapter 3. See if you've got a market for it. If you have, you've got to create something for people to look at – an eBook, a webinar, a short course proposal, a sample, a prototype of some sort.

It really doesn't matter how perfect it is; just create something so that you can get feedback. Then, get it out to the world – send an email asking friends to review it, ask a mentor to comment on it, attend a networking event and offer it to the delegates for free, write a blog post about it, create a one-page website and take out a pay-per-click ad to drive traffic to the page to ascertain interest and collect some email addresses.

Do something! Don't let the idea just fester in your head, gathering mental dust. That's a recipe for frustration and, if left too long, regret.

Action: Write down all the questions that a customer or prospect might ask about your product. Then, answer those questions. That forms the basis of your FAQ and that in turn can become your eBook, something you can give away in return for a prospect's details. You have to start somewhere, and this eBook will serve multiple purposes down the track.

Step 4: Profit

You need to know that what you're offering has a target market that's willing and able to pay your price; that the demand for what you offer is in a growth phase; that you're not differentiated by being the lowest priced; and that it is difficult for others to easily replicate what you do.

Action: Google the competition. What do they offer? How much do they charge? How does your offering stack up? Can you offer something they can't? What's the most that you can charge? How can you minimise your costs? Can you create a three-tiered pricing structure so that no matter what your market's budget, you have something to offer them? Then, nominate a price and offer it to your audience and see what happens. You can 'pivot' from there.

Step 5: Positioning

You need to demonstrate credibility; provide third-party proof that you are as good as you say; answer every question the consumer has about the product (before they buy it); make it easy for them to buy; offer an iron-clad money-back guarantee and prove that you are a legitimate business.

Action: Start collecting testimonials as soon as possible. Video them if you can, but if you can't, or it's easier, send an email or a LinkedIn request asking for one. Remember, it may feel torturous to ask, but for a short burst of pain, you get a long term gain. Send them some dot points you'd like to cover so that they know what to write.

If you've got a website, make sure you have lots of product photos, clear directions on how customers can contact you and a step-by-step process that makes it clear how and what they can buy from you. Put industry and association logos on your website, offer a 100 per cent money-back guarantee and put the eBook of FAQs you created up on your website.

Step 6: Profile

You need to have an online identity that reflects who you want to be and how you want to be seen; a library of great content that operates 24/7 selling your business while you can't; and a website that ranks well on Google.

Action: Google yourself. What comes up? If you don't like what you see, get active and start creating keyword-rich content that will push those other results down, and your content up. Write blogs, offer them to your industry associations for publishing and remember to add a brief biography at the end, with your contact details plainly listed and a link to your site.

Get really good at public speaking — it's the fastest way to build your credibility and influence. Ask around at networking groups if you can do a talk on your topic.

Write a media release and target it at a specific paper or journalist. Visualise the story you'd like to read and retrofit the media release accordingly so that the journalist can just cut and paste your release as their story.

Step 7: Promotion

You need to be able to market your business using PR, print, social media, events, email and content marketing.

Action: Build a website for your personal or business brand. Here's a tip — after you've had a go and discovered that it's harder than it looks, get an outsourced provider to give you a hand. It will be money well spent. Getting a website off the ground can really set you back time-wise, so don't wait for perfection — just get something up. And don't forget the ABC of online marketing — Always Be Collecting email addresses. Remember, if you want dozens of customers, you have to start with one. Just use Excel as your database package to start with. With a small list there's no need to buy fancy-pancy database packages.

* * *

I could go on. But I won't. What I will do is invite you to contact me and become part of our community. We regularly run webinars, events, training courses and mentoring programmes that will help you take this information, put it into practice, and hold you accountable.

If you'd like to learn more specifically about creating a new online business, or amplifying your online footprint for your existing business, you can enrol in our Secrets of Aussie Online Entrepreneurs Coaching Academy. This online course mirrors the seven-step process laid out in this book.

To learn more about it, download your free three-part video series – Getting Started As An Online Entrepreneur – by heading over to:

Secrets of Aussie Online Entrepreneurs Coaching Academy

Web: www.bernadetteschwerdt.com.au
Email: info@copyschool.com
Facebook: https://www.facebook.com/AussieOnlineEntrepreneurs
Twitter: https://twitter.com/OzBizSecrets

Copywriting Courses for Entrepreneurs

To learn how to write great content for your profiles, blogs, websites, videos and more, enrol in one of our Australian School of Copywriting courses.

Web: www.copyschool.com
Email: info@copyschool.com
Facebook: https://www.facebook.com/copyschool

APPENDIX 1

THE TOP FREE APPS EVERY ONLINE ENTREPRENEUR NEEDS WHEN STARTING OUT

Here is a list of free apps and websites you can use to help you set up your online business (see table A1, overleaf).

Take a quick look at what each offers and you'll discover very quickly that herein lies gold! Instead of having to work out which services you'll need, you can take it from me and the entrepreneurs that many of these apps and services are 'must haves' for any online business.

Having this list at your fingertips will save you hours of research. Just see what's on offer here and cherry-pick the services that are of value to you. All of them are free and if you like them but want to really maximise their functionality, you can upgrade to a paid service.

But I can tell you right now that if you're just starting out, these services will suffice for some time to come and will get you over those early humps and hurdles that make setting up a new business so hard.

Good luck!

Please note all URLs and prices were correct at the time of printing.

Table A1: the top free apps and websites for your online business

App/Software	Website	Description	Paid/Free
Dropbox	www.dropbox.com	A free service that lets you take your photos, docs and videos anywhere and share them easily	Dropbox Basic accounts start with 2GB of free space
Hightail	www.hightail.com	Online file sharing, storage and much more	Hightail offers a Free account with a 2GB online drive
MailChimp	www.mailchimp.com	Online email-marketing solution to manage contacts, send emails and track results Offers plug-ins for other programs Sends automated emails based on customer behaviour and preferences Has automation and personalisation	You can send 12 000 emails a month to a list of up to 2000 subscribers with MailChimp's Forever Free plan
Evernote	www.evernote.com	A place where you can write free from distraction, collect information, find what you need and present your ideas to the world	Free: Upload up to 60MB of data each month, with unlimited storage
vimeo	vimeo.com	A video-sharing platform for amateurs and professionals alike To upload, share, connect, explore and learn	Free: Storage up to 0.5GB a week, but with limited features

Camtasia	www.techsmith.com	Camtasia Studio and Camtasia for Mac creates video tutorials and presentations directly via screencast, or via a direct recording plug-in to Microsoft PowerPoint	Camtasia offers a free 30-day trial with certain limitations
WordPress	www.wordpress.org	Web software you can use to create a beautiful website or blog Has also evolved to be a viable content management system (CMS) for easy sharing and publishing of information	Free hosting for a blog or information-based website from their templates Software script can also be freely downloaded and installed onto your own web host
VoiceMemo	https://voice-memos.appspot.com/	VoiceMemo is a simple voice recorder that quickly records audio notes and plays them back (with pause/resume) with a single click on the list entry, identified by the date/time of the recording	Free
Nuance Dragon Dictation	www.nuance.com	Dictate a text message or email, create Facebook status updates or a tweet Simply speak and see your text content appear	Free
mockingbird	www.gomockingbird.com	An online tool that makes it easy for you to create, link together, preview, and share mock-ups of your website or application	Free to try

(continued)

Table A1: the top free apps and websites for your online business *(cont'd)*

App/Software	Website	Description	Paid/Free
Wix	www.wix.com	A free, user-friendly, website-building platform to help you create amazing, professional looking sites, which can be updated and edited easily No technical skills are required and sites are 100 per cent search-engine friendly Offers a wide range of site templates, or you can build your site from scratch	Free until you want to have your own domain name and remove Wix ads
weebly	www.weebly.com	Easy and affordable way to create a site that is unique Start your own business, communicate with your clients, showcase your achievements and be an authority on personal and professional interests	Basic package is free, but will include a small Weebly ad in your website's footer Starter: small fee lets you fully customise Pro plan: monthly charge Business: monthly charge with unlimited number of products and features
Sequoia Open Source ERP	freecode. com/projects/ sequoiaerp	An ERP suite that offers e-commerce, point of sale, inventory, warehouse, manufacturing, customer service and content management applications Written in Java, can be deployed on Linux/ Unix and Windows, and is compatible with MySQL, PostgreSQL, Oracle, Microsoft SQL Server and most other major relational databases	Open source: 100% free to download, install and customise

App	URL	Description	Pricing
odoo	www.odoo.com	Suite of open-source apps, ERP, website builder, e-commerce, point of sale and business intelligence	Free for One App with less than 50 users
PostgreSQL (database)	www.postgresql.org	The official site for PostgreSQL, the world's most advanced open-source database	Open source: 100% free to download, install and customise
inFlow	www.inflowinventory.com	An inventory system for small- to mid-sized businesses to handle sales, purchasing and inventory management and control	Free for 100 products and customers; Can upgrade for unlimited products
7-Zip (file archiver)	www.7-zip.org	An open-source file archiver with a high compression ratio, GUI and command line options	Free to download and use
Comodo (antivirus and internet security)	www.comodo.com	Offers 360° protection by combining powerful antivirus protection, an enterprise-class packet filtering firewall, advanced host intrusion prevention and automatic sandboxing of unknown files	Free to download and use; Pro version: annual charge for advanced support
box	www.box.com	Offers free cloud storage and file-sharing services that enable you to securely share and access files online	Free trial for up to 10GB
TeamViewer	www.teamviewer.com/hi/index.aspx	Connects to any PC or server around the world within a few seconds; You can remote control your partner's PC as if you were sitting right in front of it	Free for all non-commercial users; chargeable for commercial purposes

(continued)

Table A1: the top free apps and websites for your online business *(cont'd)*

App/Software	Website	Description	Paid/Free
OpenOffice	www.openoffice.org	Open-source office software suite for word processing, spreadsheets, databases, graphics, presentations and more	Open source: 100% free to download, install and customise
Mozilla Thunderbird	www.mozilla.org/en-US/thunderbird	Thunderbird is a free email application Mozilla Thunderbird is created by a global non-profit dedicated to putting individuals in control and shaping the future of the web for the public good	Open source: 100% free to download, install and customise
Mozilla Lightning Calendar	www.mozilla.org/en-US/projects/calendar	Organise your schedule and life's important events in a calendar that's fully integrated with your Thunderbird or Seamonkey email Manage multiple calendars, create your daily to-do list, invite friends to events and subscribe to public calendars	Open source: 100% free to download, install and customise
TurboCASH (accounting package)	www.turbocash.net	An SME accounting package that will make your business competitive	Open source: 100% free to download, install and customise
Speek	www.speek.com	A free conferencing service that works via the web or with the iPhone or Android phones Schedule and create conference calls, send out invitations, see your history of conference calls, share files and messages, and more for free	Free, unlimited conference calls for up to 5 guests

			Free trial available
Expensify	www.expensify.com	Handles all aspects of expense tracking on the iPhone	
		An image of a receipt can be snapped in the app and expenses can be imported from bank statements online	
		Expense entries can be automatically entered by forwarding copies of emailed receipts to your Expensify online account	
Intuit Snap Payroll	www.snappayroll.intuit.com	Calculates how much to pay employees based on the number of hours they work, how much to deduct in taxes, and so on	Free 30-day trial available
		Enter the work hours, the pay rate, the state where you have your business and this app does the rest	
		Lets you check the history of the payroll cheques you've written	
Scribus (desktop publishing)	www.scribus.net	An open-source program that brings professional page layout to Linux, BSD UNIX, Solaris and Windows	Open source: 100% free to download, install and customise
		Supports professional publishing features, such as colour separations, CMYK and spot colours, ICC colour management and versatile PDF creation	

(continued)

Table A1: the top free apps and websites for your online business *(cont'd)*

App/Software	Website	Description	Paid/Free
Square	www.squareup.com	A payment app that uses a small, portable credit/debit card reader to help make transactions fast and convenient Perfect for businesses like food trucks where space is limited.	Free for Android and ioS
SimpleInvoices	www .simpleinvoices.org	A free, open-source, web-based invoicing system that you can install on your server/PC or have hosted by one of their service providers Easily track your finances, send invoices as PDFs and many other great features	Open source: 100% free to download, install and customise

APPENDIX 2
THE COPYWRITER'S CREATIVE BRIEF

Creative brief	
Job title	
Client name	Client contact
Product/service	
Description of product/service	
Date required	
Task: What needs to be made?	
Background to this job: Why are we advertising? Why is this piece needed?	
Objectives: What do you want to achieve? (Needs to be a specific, measureable goal)	

(continued)

Target market: You may have more than one target market. Please nominate them in order of importance to you. Please be as specific as possible about the 'person' you are targeting, not just the type of industry/company.

Features and benefits:

What will this service/product do for your customers? How will it make their life easier/richer/happier?

Feature:

Benefit:

Feature:

Benefit:

Feature:

Benefit:

Creative proposition/single-minded proposition (What's the most important message you want to leave in the consumer's mind?):

Supporting evidence/proof of claim (what testimonials, examples, awards, accolades etc can you supply?):

Tone of voice/product personality: Nominate 3 or 4 words to describe the 'voice' of the communication piece, e.g. warm, friendly, officious, classy, blue collar

Call to action: What do you want the reader to do as a result of reading your site (e.g. call you, take up an offer, email you, ask for a quote, ask for a meeting)

The offer/incentive: What can you offer the reader that will compel them to consider you (rather than the competitors)? It needs to be of high value and relevance but low cost (e.g. free report, free audit, free consultation, free DVD)

Campaign timing: Is it seasonal? Is there a theme that needs to be incorporated into the piece?

Essential requirements/mandatories: What must appear on the piece (e.g. trademarks, logos, disclaimers)? Please list here in the correct wording.

Constraints: What can't we say or mention?

Competitors: Please nominate 3 competitors and their sites that you perceive to be in direct competition with you.

1.

2.

3.

INDEX

LEARN HOW TO WRITE COPY THAT GETS RESULTS

IT'S A FACT.
GREAT COPY LEADS
TO HIGHER SALES.

- Want to learn how to write web copy, blogs, sales letters and more?

- Tired of writing copy that never converts?

- Want the formulas, templates and checklists all great copywriters use to write compelling content?

Did you know that most professional copywriters use formulas and templates to write their copy? If you'd like to get a swipe file of the top 20 formulas, tips and templates the world's most successful copywriters use then download this free report now.

Download the free 10-page report:
'The Top 20 Copywriting Formulas, Tips and Templates'

www.bernadetteschwerdt.com.au/howtowrite

Connect
with WILEY ▶▶▶

WILEY

Browse and purchase the full range of Wiley publications on our official website.

www.wiley.com

Check out the Wiley blog for news, articles and information from Wiley and our authors.

www.wileybizaus.com

Join the conversation on Twitter and keep up to date on the latest news and events in business.

@WileyBizAus

Sign up for Wiley newsletters to learn about our latest publications, upcoming events and conferences, and discounts available to our customers.

www.wiley.com/email

Wiley titles are also produced in e-book formats. Available from all good retailers.

WILEY

Learn more with practical advice from our experts

Printed in Australia
28 Jul 2016
484944